I0427806

Prepared in cooperation with the Northern Shenandoah Valley Regional Commission, Central Shenandoah Valley Planning District Commission, and Virginia Commonwealth University

South Fork Shenandoah River Habitat-Flow Modeling to Determine Ecological and Recreational Characteristics during Low-Flow Periods

Scientific Investigations Report 2012–5081

U.S. Department of the Interior
U.S. Geological Survey

South Fork Shenandoah River Habitat-Flow Modeling to Determine Ecological and Recreational Characteristics during Low-Flow Periods

By Jennifer L. Krstolic and R. Clay Ramey

Prepared in cooperation with the
Northern Shenandoah Valley Regional Commission,
Central Shenandoah Valley Planning District Commission, and
Virginia Commonwealth University

Scientific Investigations Report 2012–5081

U.S. Department of the Interior
U.S. Geological Survey

U.S. Department of the Interior
KEN SALAZAR, Secretary

U.S. Geological Survey
Marcia K. McNutt, Director

U.S. Geological Survey, Reston, Virginia: 2012

For more information on the USGS—the Federal source for science about the Earth, its natural and living resources, natural hazards, and the environment, visit *http://www.usgs.gov* or call 1-888-ASK-USGS

For an overview of USGS information products, including maps, imagery, and publications, visit *http://www.usgs.gov/pubprod*

To order this and other USGS information products, visit *http://store.usgs.gov*

Suggested citation:

Krstolic, J.L., and Ramey, R.C., 2012, South Fork Shenandoah River habitat-flow modeling to determine ecological and recreational characteristics during low-flow periods: U.S. Geological Survey Scientific Investigations Report 2012–5081, 64 p. (Available online at *http://pubs.usgs.gov/sir/2012/5081/*.)

ISBN   978–1–4113–3419–9

Acknowledgments

The authors thank the cooperators, Northern Shenandoah Valley Regional Commission and Central Shenandoah Planning District and localities therein, for support of this scientific work. Virginia Commonwealth University contributed equipment, travel funds, and supplies as well as in-kind services for this cooperative investigation to develop the fish habitat-suitability criteria. The continued interest and feedback received from policymakers, planners, utility managers, State agency staff, and private citizens enhanced the study process.

Appreciation is extended to local landowners for allowing access to the river from their properties. John Gibson of the Downriver Canoe Company allowed access to the campgrounds that accommodated the field staff. Vital field assistance was provided by our lead technician for the project, Dennis Adams (USGS, Marion, Virginia) as well as volunteers from nonprofit organizations, State agencies, universities, and private citizens. Thanks to field volunteers: Jeff Kelble (Shenandoah River Keeper), Matt Balazik (Virginia Commonwealth University), Charlie Simmons (Virginia Department of Environmental Quality), Jon Campbell (U.S. Geological Survey, Reston, Virginia), and private citizen volunteers: Julie Ramey, Gene Ramey, Chet Ramey, and Frederic Bogar. The authors thank the peer reviewers who increased the effectiveness of this document.

Contents

Figures

Tables

Conversion Factors

Inch/Pound to SI

Multiply	By	To obtain
Length		
foot (ft)	0.3048	meter (m)
mile (mi)	1.609	kilometer (km)
Area		
square mile (mi^2)	2.590	square kilometer (km^2)
Flow rate		
foot per second (ft/s)	0.3048	meter per second (m/s)
cubic foot per second (ft^3/s)	0.02832	cubic meter per second (m^3/s)
foot per mile (ft/mi)	0.1894	meter per mile (m/km)
million gallons per day (Mgal/d)	0.04381	cubic meter per second (m^3/s)

Vertical coordinate information is referenced to the North American Vertical Datum of 1988 (NAVD 88).

Horizontal coordinate information is referenced to the North American Datum of 1983 (NAD 83).

Acronyms and Abbreviations

ADCP	Acoustic Doppler Current Profiler
GPS	global positioning system
HABSIM	Habitat Simulation model
HSC	habitat-suitability criteria
JAS	July, August, September low-flow period. Signifies statistics were calculated only based on data for those 3 months over the period of record
PHABSIM	Physical Habitat Simulation model
RHABSIM	River Habitat Simulation model
USGS	U.S. Geological Survey
VAF	velocity adjustment factor
WSL	water-surface level
WUA	weighted usable-habitat area (per 1,000 feet of stream)

x

South Fork Shenandoah River Habitat-Flow Modeling to Determine Ecological and Recreational Characteristics during Low-Flow Periods

By Jennifer L. Krstolic[1] and R. Clay Ramey[2]

Abstract

The ecological habitat requirements of aquatic organisms and recreational streamflow requirements of the South Fork Shenandoah River were investigated by the U.S. Geological Survey in cooperation with the Central Shenandoah Valley Planning District Commission, the Northern Shenandoah Valley Regional Commission, and Virginia Commonwealth University. Physical habitat simulation modeling was conducted to examine flow as a major determinant of physical habitat availability and recreation suitability using field-collected hydraulic habitat variables such as water depth, water velocity, and substrate characteristics. Fish habitat-suitability criteria specific to the South Fork Shenandoah River were developed for sub-adult and adult smallmouth bass (*Micropterus dolomieu*), juvenile and sub-adult redbreast sunfish (*Lepomis auritus*), spotfin or satinfin shiner (*Cyprinella* spp.), margined madtom (*Noturus insignis*), and river chub (*Nocomis micropogon*). Historic streamflow statistics for the summer low-flow period during July, August, and September were used as benchmark low-flow conditions and compared to habitat simulation results and water-withdrawal scenarios based on 2005 withdrawal data.

To examine habitat and recreation characteristics during droughts, daily fish habitat or recreation suitability values were simulated for 2002 and other selected drought years. Recreation suitability during droughts was extremely low, because the modeling demonstrated that suitable conditions occur when the streamflows are greater than the 50th percentile flow for July, August, and September. Habitat availability for fish is generally at a maximum when streamflows are between the 75th and 25th percentile flows for July, August, and September. Time-series results for drought years, such as 2002, showed that extreme low-flow conditions less than the 5th percentile of flow for July, August, and September corresponded to below-normal habitat availability for both game and nongame fish in the upper section of the river. For the middle section near Luray, margined madtom and river chub habitat area were below normal, whereas adult and sub-adult smallmouth bass habitat area remained near the median expected available habitat. In the lower section near Front Royal, time-series results for adult smallmouth bass, sub-adult smallmouth bass, and margined madtom habitat were below normal when streamflows were below the 10th percentile flow for July, August, and September. All other species of fish had habitat availability within the normal range for July, August, and September.

Water-conservation scenarios representing a 50-percent water-withdrawal reduction resulted in game fish habitat availability within the normal range for habitat in upper and middle river sections, instead of below normal conditions which were observed during the 2002 drought. The 50-percent water-withdrawal reduction had no measurable effect on

[1]U.S. Geological Survey, Richmond, Virginia.

[2]Virginia Commonwealth University, Richmond, Virginia, and ETI Professionals, Denver, Colorado.

recreation. For nongame fish such as river chub, a 20-percent withdrawal reduction resulted in habitat availability within the normal range for habitat in the upper and middle river sections. Increased water-use scenarios representing a 5-percent increase in water withdrawals resulted in a slight reduction in habitat availability; however, increased withdrawals of 20 and 50 percent resulted in habitat availability substantially less than the 25th habitat percentile, or below normal. Habitat reductions were more pronounced when flows were lower than the 10th percentile flow for July, August, and September.

The results show that for normal or wet years, increased water withdrawals are not likely to correspond with extensive habitat loss for game fish or nongame fish. During drought years, however, a 20- to 50-percent increase in water withdrawals may result in below normal habitat availability for game fish throughout the river and nongame fish in the upper and middle sections of the river. These simulations of rare historic drought conditions, such as those observed in 2002, serve as a baseline for development of ecological flow thresholds for drought planning.

Introduction

The South Fork Shenandoah River (referred to as the South Fork in this report), and its counterpart, the North Fork Shenandoah River (referred to as the North Fork), join to form the Shenandoah River, which drains an area that many in Virginia refer to as "the Valley." With Shenandoah National Park to the east, and Massanutten Mountain to the west, the South Fork Basin is an area with much beauty, attracting new visitors and residents, many of whom are outdoor enthusiasts, tourists, and farmers. As population growth continues and new industries increase in the Valley, competition for clean water is a concern for policy makers, managers, planners, and citizens in the area who recognize the need to monitor and protect the South Fork streamflow as a resource for water supply, recreation such as canoeing, and ecological habitat for aquatic life. In 2005, the U.S. Geological Survey (USGS), in coopera-tion with the Central Shenandoah Valley Planning District Commission, the Northern Shenandoah Valley Regional Commission, and Virginia Commonwealth University, began an investigation to examine the instream flow needs of aquatic organisms of the South Fork as a companion study to the instream flow study on the North Fork (Krstolic and others 2006). As a result of the current investigation, the counties and communities in the South Fork Basin should gain knowledge of the water resources in the basin, the availability of water for fish habitat and canoeing, and the potential effects of with-drawals and conservation measures on the ecology, recreation, agriculture, industry, and water supply.

The study design was patterned after the North Fork study to provide consistent modeling output for Valley plan-ners and water-resource managers. Flow data and physical

habitat data were collected at permanent cross sections representing habitat types in the South Fork. These flow data were input to the River Habitat Simulation Software model (RHABSIM), a 1-dimensional water-surface-profile model that uses stage-discharge ratings to simulate habitat condi-tions over a range of streamflows. The modeling was used to determine the relation between suitable habitat and stream-flow. This report completes the modeling for the two major tributaries of the Shenandoah River, providing consistent results to planning district personnel toward effective drought preparation in the planning districts that span both watersheds.

The use of RHABSIM (or the original Physical Habitat Simulation model; PHABSIM) has been widespread throughout the past 30 years as part of the instream-flow incremental methodology approach to river management (Stalnaker, 1979). In fact, RHABSIM techniques for water-resources management have been used in the deci-sion making process in more than 20 countries, because the model incorporates ecological variables toward realistic outcomes (Tharme, 2003; Petts, 2009). The instream-flow incremental methodology approach to river management can use RHABSIM to explicitly link physical habitat simulation with habitat-suitability criteria for species and life stages to display the relations between habitat usability and flow (Petts, 2009). The method relies on three principles that are important to this investigation: (1) the chosen species exhibits preferences within a range of habitat conditions that it can tolerate, (2) these ranges can be defined for each species or life stage, and (3) the area of stream providing these condi-tions can be quantified as a function of discharge and channel structure (Petts, 2009). Other modeling and data-collection platforms were considered as the study was being designed in 2005. A two-dimensional modeling approach was consid-ered; however, the shallow, wide dimensions of the South Fork limited the acoustic velocity instrumentation that was available. Instruments that function in depths shallower than 2 feet (ft) were not coupled with global positioning system (GPS) technology to spatially quantify the velocity fields. Because of the need to collect spatially relevant velocity data, traditional RHABSIM data-collection methods were selected.

The association between flow variability and the health of river ecosystems is not a simple relation, because the linkages are complex in both time and space (Petts, 2009). The complexity of the relation has brought about criticism for the instream-flow incremental methodology approach for water-resources management. This is especially true when minimum flows are developed for a single species, according to Annear and others (2002), who emphasize that a single flow value (minimum, optimal, or otherwise) cannot simultaneously meet the requirements for all species or maintain a fishery. This investigation was begun under specific assumptions about fish habitat use during low-flow condi-tions, so findings are only applicable to that part of the flow regime. The applicability of the RHABSIM modeling results for high-flow periods or those related to reproduction or other physiological functions was not evaluated. A variety of species and life stages of both game and nongame warm-water fishes were evaluated for development of habitat-suitability criteria (HSC) so that modeling results would be representative of a broad range of species habitat needs. Ideally, the fish-community population size and age distribution would be monitored throughout the duration of the study, or a long-term fish community dataset would be available for all game and nongame species and linked with streamflow statistics. Neither option was entirely possible given study-scope limitations. However, a thorough evaluation of fish habitat use during the low-flow period was completed during June 2008 through September 2008. The flows during that time period were between the 50th and 75th historic monthly percentiles in June and September but were between the 10th and 25th historic monthly percentiles for July and August. These flows represent normal flows and below-normal flows, respectively.

A key assumption of this investigation and many others is that flow is a major determinant of physical habitat in rivers, which in turn is a major determinant of biotic composition (Bunn and Arthington, 2002). Another assumption is that physical habitat is a limiting factor for fish populations. Other factors that can determine whether or not fish occupancy increases or decreases with physical habitat availability are water quality, predation, competition, food availability, and disease. If other factors that were not studied on the South Fork have a greater effect on population success, then managing water supply for habitat may not promote populations. It should be emphasized that the key variables being evaluated by the RHABSIM model are components of hydraulic habitat (water depths, water velocities, and substrate characteristics) and discharge. For a study that is focused on water availability and habitat availability during drought, the approach represents a surrogate for biological response fundamental to an organism's existence (Annear and others, 2002). This approach is powerful, because it links fish habitat availability (in this case) to discharge (Annear and others, 2002) and water withdrawals. Discharge and water withdrawals are the variables that are commonly used by water-resource managers and planners, thereby making modeling results more easily applied. No dam building or human engineering and alteration of the channel form, excluding those occurring with natural floods, have occurred in the past 20 to 30 years. Therefore, an assumption can be made that no net changes due to physical alteration of habitat are occurring on the South Fork. The results of the RHABSIM modeling were used in time-series scenarios that predict habitat duration or availability typical of historic and drought streamflow conditions (1930–2008) in the South Fork. These scenarios should assist managers in selecting future thresholds for discharge and habitat that are protective of aquatic organisms and that provide water supply for human and industrial use in the South Fork Shenandoah River watershed.

Purpose and Scope

The purpose of this report is to describe the methods, document results, and discuss implications of flow habitat modeling for the South Fork Shenandoah River in Virginia. A range of scenarios is presented to provide managers and planners with information regarding current and future water resources in the basin, the availability of water for fish habitat, recreation, and the potential effects of withdrawals and conservation measures on fish populations in the South Fork. The objectives of this investigation are to enhance the understanding of summer low-flow conditions in the South Fork relative to the physical habitat needs of fish, and to analyze water use and recreation needs of humans, such as canoeing conditions along certain stream riffles. Specifically, study objectives were to incorporate mesoscale and microscale physical habitat information and detailed streamflow data into 1-dimensional physical habitat models to quantify availability of suitable fish habitat during low-flow conditions, as well as to develop water-use and water-conservation scenarios for current and future water withdrawals that might affect aquatic habitat.

Study Area

The South Fork Shenandoah River and its watershed are the main focus of this investigation. The watershed begins in Augusta County, Virginia (Va.) by three main tributaries—the North, Middle, and South Rivers—which merge to form the South Fork near Lynnwood, Va. The South Fork flows north 97 miles (mi) to meet the North Fork Shenandoah River at the Town of Front Royal (Virginia Department of Game and Inland Fisheries, 2011) (fig. 1). The South Fork is a typical low-gradient stream with a main channel slope that ranges from 3.84 to 0.55 feet per mile (ft/mi) from upstream to downstream (Austin and others, 2011), and has an average basin slope that ranges from 290 to 306 ft/mi (Paybins, 2008; Austin and others, 2011). Average basin slope is measured by summing the length of all elevation contours in miles, multiplied by the 20-ft contour interval, then divided by the square mileage of the drainage area (Harvey and Eash, 1996; Paybins, 2008; Austin and others, 2011). The South Fork is a typical low-gradient stream with a main channel slope that ranges from 3.84 to 0.55 ft/mi from upstream to downstream (Austin and others, 2011), and has an average basin slope that ranges from 290 to 306 ft/mi (Paybins, 2008; Austin and others, 2011), but it does have some Class I and Class II rapids (Virginia Department of Game and Inland Fisheries, 2011). The 1,634-square mile (mi^2) watershed generally is long and narrow, as it is confined over most of its length by the Blue Ridge Mountains to the east and Massanutten Mountain to the west.

Land use in the South Fork watershed above Front Royal is primarily forest (55 percent), grass or pasture (30 percent), urban (11 percent), and row-crop agriculture (4 percent) (Multi-Resolution Land Characteristics Consortium, 2001). The geology

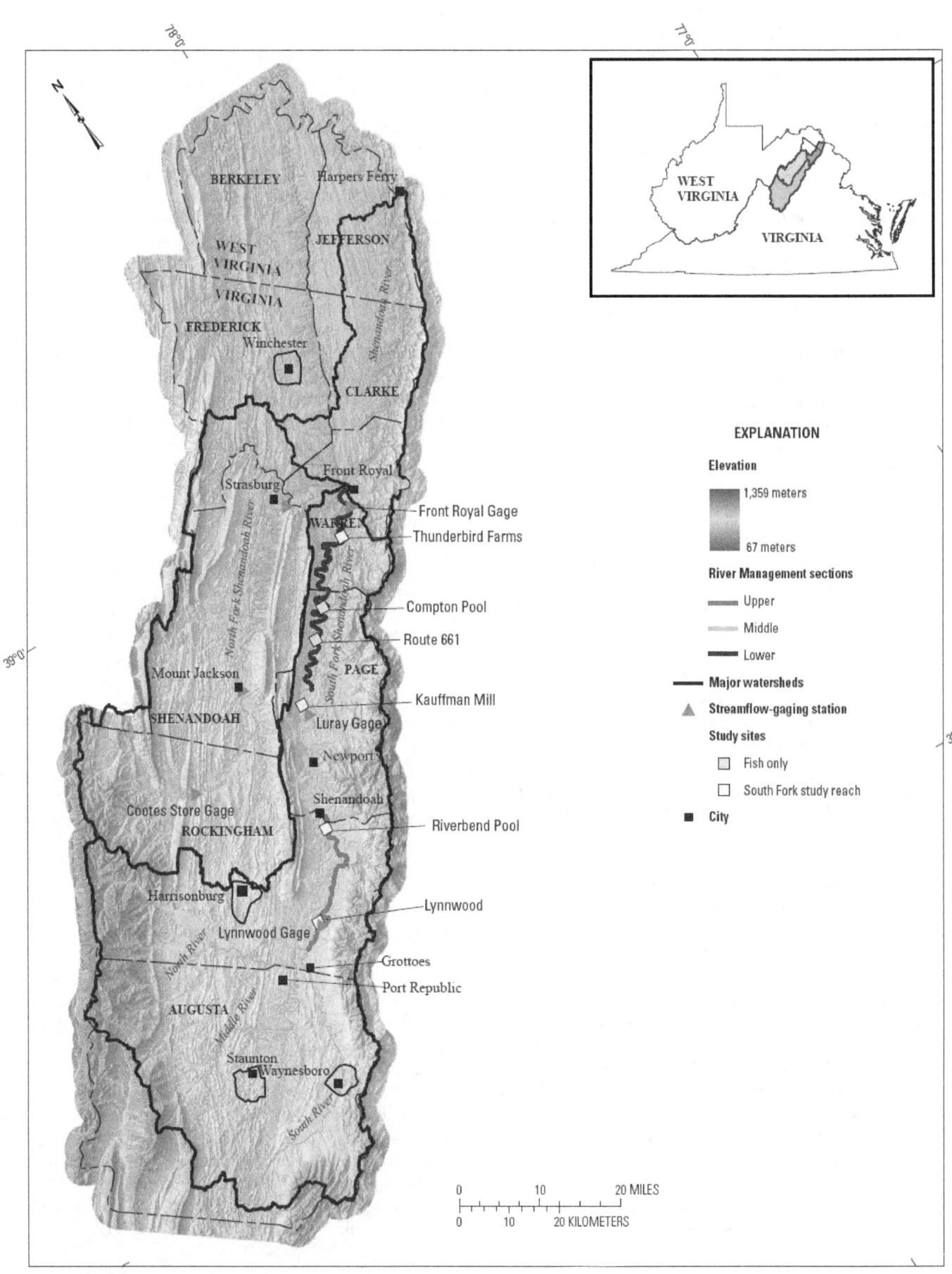

of the total upstream area of the watershed at Front Royal also is representative of the watershed segments upstream at Luray or Lynnwood. The geology consists of Blue Ridge metamorphic rock (10 percent), Valley and Ridge carbonate rock (48 percent), and Valley and Ridge silicilastic rock (41 percent) (Virginia Department of Mines, Minerals, and Energy; Division of Mineral Resources, 2005; Austin and others, 2011). The valley bottoms are made up of sandstone, shale, and carbonate rocks (Yager and others, 2008). The ridges and hill slopes within the basin are primarily underlain by silicilastic rocks. The southern end of the basin adjacent to the Blue Ridge generally is referred to as the "western-toe carbonate unit," which is made up of carbonate rocks overlain by colluvial gravel (Yager and others, 2008). This area has depths to bedrock that are greater than other places in the Shenandoah River watershed and is an important recharge area for groundwater (Morgan and others, 2004; Swain and others, 2004; Yager and others, 2008).

Using the National Hydrography Dataset for reporting study results, the South Fork, beginning near Port Republic, was divided into upper (0 to 25 river miles), middle (26 to 55 river miles), and lower (56 to 106 river miles) sections (fig. 1). Each of these sections ends at a hydrogeomorphic discontinuity (Larned and others, 2010), either manmade impoundments or a river confluence. Streamflow-gaging stations are located within each section: South Fork Shenandoah River near Lynnwood (01628500), South Fork Shenandoah River near Luray (01629500), and South Fork Shenandoah River at Front Royal (01631000) (fig. 1, table 1).

Analysis of Historic Streamflow

Streamflows of the South Fork have been monitored for at least 79 years by the USGS and the Virginia Department of Environmental Quality. The long-term records from three streamflow-gaging stations (table 1) can be used to characterize the flow regime (seasonal, monthly, and annual patterns) of the South Fork that may affect water availability and habitat for aquatic species. The period of record for the Front Royal and Lynnwood streamflow-gaging stations include data from 1931 and 1930, respectively, to the present. A continuous record for the Luray streamflow-gaging station is only available from 1925 to 1951 and from 1979 to the present (only the more recent period at the Luray gage was used in this study). Records from these three streamflow-gaging stations were used to represent the variation in statistics longitudinally as the drainage area increases. Long-term streamflow data from these three stations provide an opportunity to characterize dry, wet, and normal years, and subsequently, to assess fish habitat availability during these contrasting conditions. Water is withdrawn for a variety of uses from the South Fork as well as three power-supply dams that represent nonconsumptive water use. During extreme low-flow periods, dam releases may be evident in the streamflow record; however, the dams are generally flow-over spillways that do not commonly alter the natural flow regime of the river.

Table 1. Selected streamflow-gaging stations in the Shenandoah River Basin, Virginia.

[SF, South Fork]

Station number	Station name	Drainage area, square miles	Operating agency	Period of record
01628500	SF Shenandoah River near Lynnwood	1,079	Virginia Department of Environmental Quality	1930–2008
01629500	SF Shenandoah River near Luray	1,372	Virginia Department of Environmental Quality	1979–2008
01631000	SF Shenandoah River at Front Royal	1,634	U.S. Geological Survey	1931–2008

Map credit—

Elevation from U.S. Geological Survey National Elevation Data Set digital elevation model, 2005, 10-meter resolution
Universal Transverse Mercator 17 projection, NAD 83, central meridian -81 00'W, rotated 30 degrees
Hydrography from U. S. Geological Survey National Hydrography Dataset, accessed 2007, 1:24,000;
City location from U. S. Census Cartographic Boundary Files, Consolidated Cities, 2000, ~ 1:500,000
Watershed boundaries from Krstolic, 2007, Drainage basin delineations for selected USGS streamflow-gaging stations in Virginia

Figure 1. *At left*—South Fork Shenandoah River, Virginia, watershed and study sites.

To identify critical flow components, the beginning of any hydrologic assessment includes characterization of flow time series (Larned and others, 2010), including the development of flow-duration curves, which is a summarization of streamflows grouped into percentiles. These percentiles are based on a scale of 1 to 100, and indicate the percentage of a data distribution that is equal to or below each percentile value. For example, the 90th percentile of a river is equal to or greater than 90 percent of the daily discharge values recorded during all years that measurements have been made. A discharge at the 10th percentile is equal to or greater than 10 percent of recorded daily values, making it represent the lower end of flows. In this report, the percentiles are based on historic daily values calculated for a given time period, which are typically annual records or the low-flow summer months of July, August, and September (JAS). In the recent publication of the North Fork Shenandoah River (Krstolic and others, 2006) a variation of the percentile known as the "percent exceedance" was used. Percent exceedance (Searcy, 1969) is obtained by subtracting the percentile scale value from 100 percent.

In this document, most flow units are referred to in cubic feet per second (ft^3/s), but tables and figures include million gallons per day (Mgal/d) where relevant (1 ft^3/s equals 0.6465 Mgal/d). This study primarily incorporates flow percentiles calculated on an annual basis and calculated over the summer low-flow period during JAS (table 2). For reference, the report uses the 25–75th percentile range as a "normal" condition. Table 2 shows the 25–75th percentile range for each streamflow-gaging station. Flows less than the 25th percentile represent conditions that indicate less water availability and may indicate drought as the percentiles decrease. As in the North Fork investigation (Krstolic and others, 2006), historic data from JAS are used to assess flows during the time of year when precipitation is low, temperatures are high, and water-use demands are high.

Years having flows much lower than the normal range of flows in JAS (typically 10th percentile JAS flow or lower) were classified as dry years (Krstolic and others, 2006). Typically, a 10th percentile JAS flow occurs 3 days per month; therefore, when more than 50 percent of days in a given month have a discharge below this threshold, it is an indicator that water availability is scarce. Figures 2, 3, and 4 illustrate the numbers of days per month flow decreased below the 10th percentile JAS flow during the period of record for each streamflow-gaging station. As a conservative measure to characterize drought years, the 10th percentile annual flow was considered. For the South Fork, the 10th percentile annual flow occurred an average of 69 to 96 percent of the days during JAS during drought years.

Table 2.   Streamflow statistics for gages on the South Fork Shenandoah River, Virginia.

[Annual statistics represent conditions over all months of the year for the entire period of record for each gage through 2008. July–August–September statistics represent the 3-month average flow conditions for the entire period of record through 2008. Monthly statistics are updated daily and available for each streamflow-gaging station at *http //va.water. usgs.gov/duration_plots/dp_map_potomac.htm*]

Percentile	Lynnwood 01628500	Luray 01629500	Front Royal 01631000	Lynnwood 01628500	Luray 01629500	Front Royal 01631000
	Million gallons per day			**Cubic feet per second**		
	Annual					
95	2,023	2,702	3,005	3,130	4,180	4,650
90	1,357	1,790	2,042	2,100	2,770	3,160
75	724	976	1,138	1,120	1,510	1,760
50	390	535	613	604	828	948
25	218	304	344	337	470	533
10	152	228	249	235	352	386
5	128	198	212	198	307	328
	July–August–September					
95	1,034	1,480	1,525	2,290	2,290	2,360
90	633	737	963	1,140	1,140	1,490
75	352	497	537	769	769	831
50	233	317	360	491	491	557
25	171	246	271	380	380	420
10	131	200	213	310	310	330
5	115	169	187	262	262	290

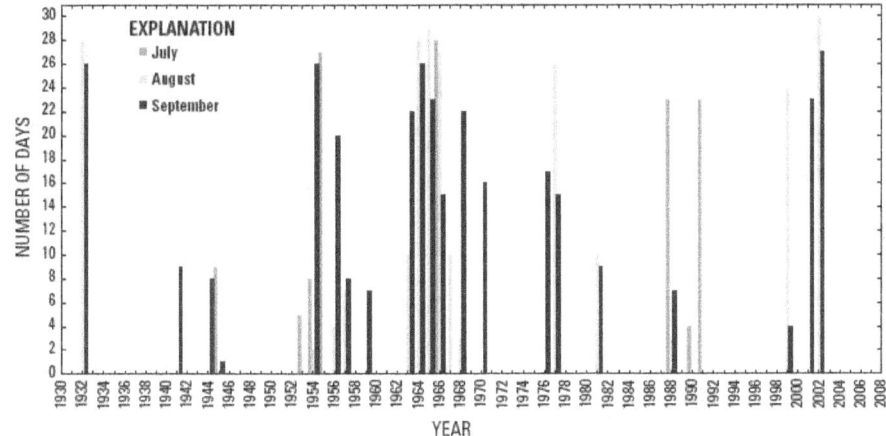

Figure 2. Number of days per month and year (1930–2008) with streamflow values less than or equal to the 10th percentile flow for July, August, and September for the Lynnwood streamflow-gaging station (01628500) on the South Fork Shenandoah River, Virginia.

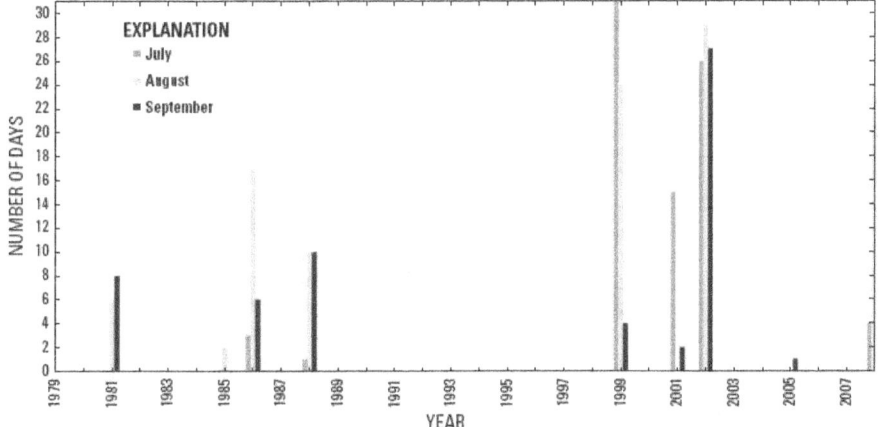

Figure 3. Number of days per month and year (1979–2008) with streamflow values less than or equal to the 10th percentile flow for July, August, and September for the Luray streamflow-gaging station (01629500) on the South Fork Shenandoah River, Virginia.

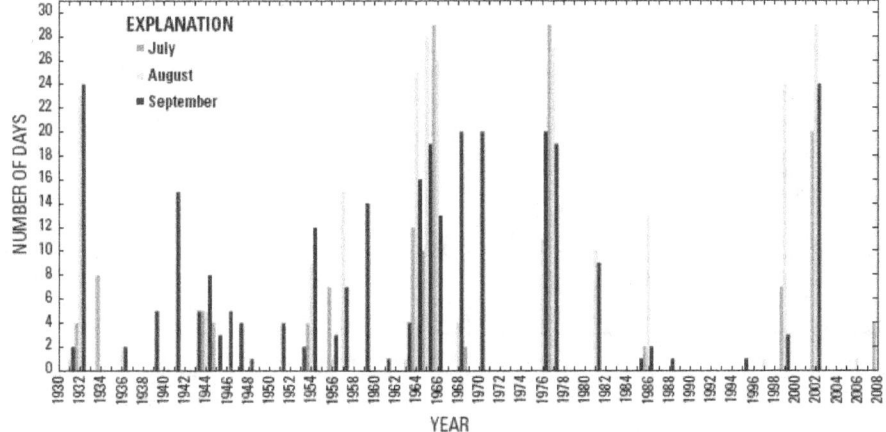

Figure 4. Number of days per month and year (1930–2008) with streamflow values less than or equal to 10th percentile flow for July, August, and September for the Front Royal streamflow-gaging station (01631000) on the South Fork Shenandoah River, Virginia.

Water Withdrawals

Water-use data for the South Fork were compiled from the most recent USGS publication available (Kenny and others, 2009). The data in this report are total withdrawals taken from the river and from groundwater for 2005, without accounting for water returns. Estimates of consumptive use compared to return flow are quite complicated and are beyond the scope of this investigation. Water-use categories in Kenny and others (2009) included location-specific withdrawal datasets, such as public-water supply, commercial industrial, thermoelectric, hydroelectric, golf course irrigation, and mining, as well as nonspatially referenced categories with water withdrawals summarized by county, including row crop irrigation, livestock, aquaculture, and domestic self-supply groundwater wells. The county-level data for row crops, livestock, aquaculture, and domestic self-supply wells were approximated, based on published methods for estimating water use (Lovelace, 2009a–c). The only category that was excluded from this summary was hydroelectric power, because the majority of the water used was returned to the river. The location-specific water-use data were summarized for comparison purposes for each major

watershed section of the South Fork in the study area, as well as for the tributaries upstream, the North Fork, and the mainstem Shenandoah River. The county-level data water-use estimates were apportioned to each watershed based on the percentage of county land area it contained and added to the location-specific water-use data (table 3). The categories of surface-water and groundwater withdrawals in the Shenandoah Valley are shown in figure 5.

Because water withdrawals from an upstream section could reduce water availability downstream, cumulative water withdrawals were calculated from upstream to downstream. For example, total water withdrawals for Luray are equal to the water withdrawals for the watershed around Luray in addition to the water withdrawals for the North, Middle, South River watersheds and the area draining to Lynnwood (fig. 5).

The largest surface-water withdrawals were located in the tributaries to the South Fork in the North (17.7 Mgal/d), Middle (10.4 Mgal/d), and South (9.8 Mgal/d) Rivers, respectively (table 3). Much of the water-use estimates for Augusta County came from aquaculture withdrawals that equaled 25.9 Mgal/d and were proportionally distributed across the

Table 3. Surface-water and groundwater withdrawals for 2005 in the Shenandoah River watershed, and cumulative withdrawals for the South Fork Shenandoah River, Virginia.

[Hydroelectric power withdrawal values were omitted because they were assumed to be 100-percent returned flow. Data[1] from Kenny and others, 2009. NF, North Fork; SF, South Fork]

Station number	Name	Million gallons per day			Cubic feet per second		
		Surface water	Ground-water	Total	Surface water	Ground-water	Total
01632000	NF Shenandoah River at Cootes Store	3.3	1.1	4.3	5.0	1.7	6.7
01633000	NF Shenandoah River at Mount Jackson	7.5	2.6	10.1	11.6	4.0	15.6
	NF Shenandoah at mouth	18.4	4.5	23.0	28.5	7.0	35.5
	South River at mouth	9.8	12.3	22.1	15.1	19.0	34.1
	Middle River at mouth	10.4	3.9	14.4	16.2	6.1	22.3
	North River at mouth	17.7	3.9	21.7	27.4	6.1	33.6
01628500	SF Shenandoah River near Lynnwood	0.4	0.1	0.6	0.7	0.2	0.9
01629500	SF Shenandoah River near Luray	3.5	13.6	17.0	5.4	21.0	26.4
	SF Shenandoah at mouth	2.4	1.7	4.0	3.6	2.6	6.2
	Shenandoah River at mouth	3.5	1.1	4.6	5.5	1.6	7.1
Total 2005 water use in the Shenandoah River watershed		76.9	44.9	121.7	119.0	69.4	188.4
Cumulative withdrawals for the South Fork Shenandoah River							
01628500	Lynnwood	38.3	20.3	58.7	59.4	31.5	90.9
01629500	Luray	41.8	33.9	75.8	64.8	52.5	117.3
01631000	Front Royal	44.5	35.6	79.8	68.4	55.1	123.5

[1]Location-specific withdrawal data including: public-water supply, commercial industrial, thermoelectric, hydroelectric, golf-course irrigation, and mining; and nonspatially referenced county-level data including: row-crop irrigation, livestock, aquaculture, and domestic self-supplied groundwater wells.

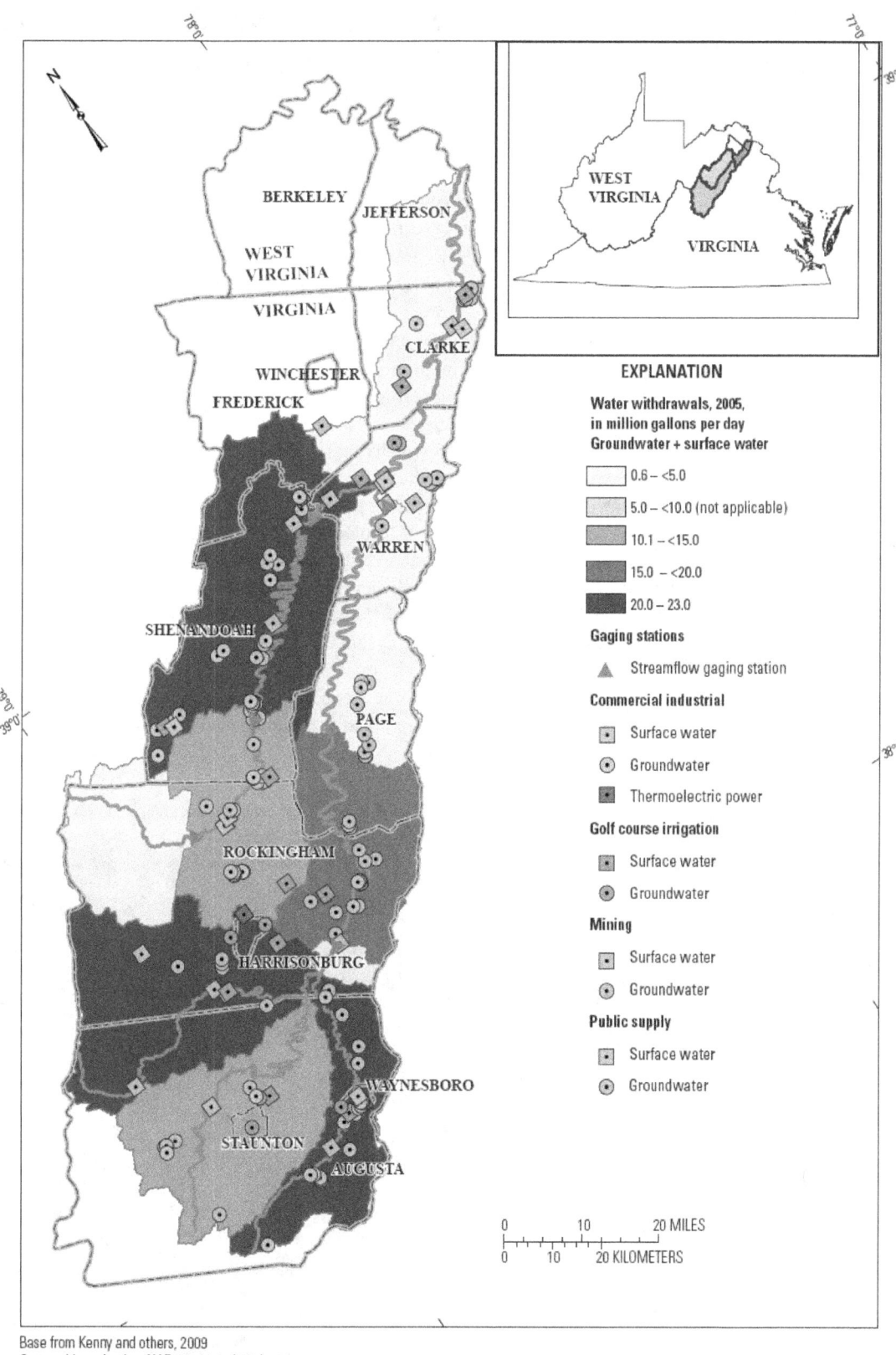

Base from Kenny and others, 2009
Geographic projection, NAD 83, rotated 36 degrees;
Virginia Department of Conservataion and Recreation, 2004, 1:24,000;
U.S. Geological Survey National Atlas coverage, 1:2,000,000

Figure 5.   Surface-water and groundwater withdrawal locations for the Shenandoah River watershed in Virginia, 2005.

watershed by area. Discharge from these rivers forms the South Fork Shenandoah River. As the river flows to Lynnwood, an additional 0.4 Mgal/d is withdrawn; at Luray, an additional 3.5 Mgal/d is withdrawn; and at the mouth of the South Fork, an additional 2.4 Mgal/d is withdrawn. The cumulative total surface-water withdrawal from the South Fork Shenandoah River was 44.5 Mgal/d (table 3), which does not account for water returns to the river. The annual median flow ranges from 390 to 612 Mgal/d for Lynnwood to Front Royal, and the summer JAS period has median flows ranging from 233 to 360 Mgal/d. During the low-flow period, the surface-water withdrawals represent 12 to 19 percent of the median flow.

Groundwater withdrawals are common in the South Fork watershed, and in a watershed that is underlain by a large amount of carbonate bedrock, the groundwater conditions are expected to be closely linked to stream conditions. A recent investigation in the Shenandoah River watershed found that source waters to tributary streams were 50- to 80-percent groundwater during dry conditions (Nelms and Moberg, 2010). Groundwater withdrawals are a substantial portion of the water used in the watershed. Groundwater withdrawals are highest in the watershed draining the South River (12.3 Mgal/d) and the watershed draining to Luray (13.6 Mgal/d), with the rest of the groundwater withdrawals coming from other parts of the South Fork watershed. The cumulative total for the South Fork watershed groundwater withdrawals is 35.6 Mgal/d (table 3).

Mesohabitat Summary of the South Fork Shenandoah River

Mesohabitats are channel-spanning, moderately large hydrogeomorphic habitat units, such as a riffle, run, or pool having relatively homogeneous channel characteristics (Vadas, 1992; Vadas and Orth, 1998; Krstolic and others, 2006). Mesohabitats for the entire South Fork were mapped during the summer in 2006 and 2007 following similar methods as the North Fork Shenandoah River (Krstolic and others, 2006) to gain an understanding of the habitat distribution during low-flow periods. Spatial data with habitat descriptor information for both rivers are available as a digital data release of Geographic Information Systems (GIS) data (Krstolic and Hayes, 2010). These data are useful for summarizing the overall habitat availability for fish in the river and serve as the basis for weighting of transect habitat types in the habitat modeling phase of this study.

Mesohabitat characteristics for the South Fork are summarized in table 4 and follow the categories presented in Krstolic and others (2006), with the addition of the habitat category "glide," to describe the downstream end of a pool where it shallows and transitions into riffle habitat (Krstolic and Hayes, 2010). Mesohabitat length throughout the South Fork consists of 52.6-percent run, 35.7-percent pool, and 11.7-percent riffle (table 4).

Bedrock riffle and aquatic vegetation, South Fork Shenandoah River

Table 4. Results of the mesohabitat classification and mapping for three sections of the South Fork Shenandoah River, Virginia.

[ND, no data]

Habitat type	Lynnwood (upper section)						Luray (middle section)						Front Royal (lower section)						Whole River					
	Number of sections	Length, miles	Percentage of total	Percentage of total by habitat type	Median width, feet	Median average depth, feet	Number of sections	Length, miles	Percentage of total	Percentage of total by habitat type	Median width, feet	Median average depth, feet	Number of sections	Length, miles	Percentage of total	Percentage of total by habitat type	Median width, feet	Median average depth, feet	Number of sections	Length, miles	Percentage of total	Percentage of total by habitat type	Median width, feet	Median average depth, feet
Particle riffle	58	1.8	9.8	7.4	172.5	0.8	38	1.6	8.3	5.4	210.0	1.0	32	1.5	14.6	2.9	300.0	0.8	128	4.9	11.7	4.6	213.0	0.8
Bedrock riffle	21	0.6		2.4	264.0	0.8	34	0.9		2.9	286.5	1.0	129	6.0		11.7	336.0	0.8	184	7.5		7.1	306.0	0.8
Particle run	97	8.1		32.8	165.0	2.0	60	5.2		17.6	226.5	2.0	59	5.2		10.1	298.5	1.7	216	18.5		17.5	210.0	2.0
Bedrock run	61	4.9	54.2	20.0	207.0	2.3	92	9.0	49.4	30.3	252.0	2.3	213	21.3	53.6	41.6	297.0	2.0	366	35.3	52.6	33.4	273.0	2.0
Pocket run	3	0.3		1.3	217.5	5.3	3	0.4		1.5	201.0	3.6	10	1.0		1.9	264.0	3.3	16	1.7		1.7	243.0	3.8
Natural pool	60	5.6		23.0	213.0	6.0	56	4.7		15.9	249.0	5.0	105	11.5		22.5	289.5	5.0	221	21.9		20.7	255.0	5.5
Artificial pool	10	1.4	36.0	5.8	301.5	8.5	41	5.7	42.3	19.1	333.0	8.8	3	0.3	31.8	0.5	306.0	4.0	54	7.4	35.7	7.0	316.5	8.5
Backwater	8	0.7		2.8	318.0	ND	11	1.1		3.7	120.0	ND	31	3.5		7.0	36.0	ND	50	5.3		5.1	105.0	ND
Glide	22	1.1		4.4	207.0	2.0	19	1.1		3.6	243.0	2.1	17	0.9		1.8	333.0	2.5	58	3.1		2.9	243.0	2.0
Totals	340	24.5	100.0	100.0			354	29.7	100.0	100.0			599	51.3	100.0	100.0			1,293	105.6	100.0	100.0		

Riffle   Shallow rapids, with fast velocities, in an open stream where a turbulent water surface is created by obstructions that are wholly or partly submerged. Water depth is generally less than 1 foot. Substrate is either bedrock or boulder, cobble, gravel, and sand (particle).

Run   Swift moving areas characterized by predominantly smooth to slightly turbulent flow. The water surface is usually flat and is not broken by the substrate. Water depth is typically 1–5 feet. Gently sloping bed with fairly consistent and uniform depth. Pocket runs shallow areas of bedrock interspersed with a mosaic of deeper holes or "pockets" that provide cover for fish. Run substrate is either bedrock with little silt and sand, or cobble, gravel, and sand.

Pool   Areas with reduced or barely perceptible surface velocity, with a smooth, unbroken water surface. Water depth is greater than 5 feet. Natural pools are formed by a naturally occurring channel obstruction such as a bedrock control, island, large gravel bar, or a meander bend, whereas artificial pools are formed by obstructions such as dams. Glides are transitional habitats as a pool shallows into riffle or run habitat.

The South Fork is a large river with an average wetted channel width of 260 ft during low flow that maintains similar channel form within each habitat type throughout most of its length. Bedrock run habitat makes up 33.4 percent of the river and is the most abundant of any habitat category (table 4). The bedrock in the South Fork is usually tilted or dipping, rather than having a flat-bottom surface, and can be described as a series of "ledges and trenches" that cross the river obliquely. As the alternating pattern of shallow to deep water in these areas makes canoeing or wading challenging, the pattern also provides a substantial amount of cover for fish, because they can hide in the deep, slower water between the bedrock ledges. A similar pattern was seen with bedrock runs and bedrock riffles. Bedrock substrates are least abundant upstream but increase in percentage downstream. Particle riffles and particle runs, however, are most abundant upstream and decrease in percentage downstream (table 4).

Natural pools make up 20.7 percent of the length of the South Fork (table 4), the second most abundant habitat type. Average depths in natural pools are consistent throughout the river, ranging from 2.8- to 20.0-ft deep, with a maximum depth of 35 ft. The median average depth in artificial pools is 8.5 ft, and the maximum depth is 18 ft (Krstolic and Hayes, 2010).

Although bedrock riffles and particle riffles only make up 11.7 percent of the overall habitat, they support many of the smaller nongame fish which serve as food for game fish. These areas offer faster water velocity, shallow depths, and diversity in substrate (gravel, cobble, boulder, and bedrock bottoms) where fish can hide and forage. Depths in bedrock riffles and particle riffles are consistent, with a median average depth of 0.8 ft (Krstolic and Hayes, 2010). The mesohabitat data are used to prioritize hydraulic monitoring reaches and to weight modeling results to represent the habitats within the entire length of the South Fork.

Hydraulic Data Collection in Predominant Mesohabitat Types

Hydraulic data were used during model calibration and simulation to develop relations between water-surface levels (WSL) and discharge and between water velocity and discharge. Data were collected on the South Fork between May 2007 and August 2009.

Study Reach Selection and Description of Transects

Study reaches were selected based on accessibility by boat or wading, variety of habitat, and distribution throughout the length of the South Fork. Study reaches are shown in figure 1 and location information is presented in table 5. Study reaches span the length of the South Fork from near the confluence of the North, Middle, and South Rivers at Lynnwood to Thunderbird Farms near the confluence with the North Fork. Four reaches were selected for hydraulic data collection. All reaches contained at least one mesohabitat, and three to five semipermanent transects (following Bovee, 1997; table 6). Verticals used in velocity, depth, and substrate measurements were spaced at 10-ft intervals along each transect (modified from Bovee, 1997).

The Lynnwood reach (figs. 1, 6), is the most upstream reach. A streamflow-gaging station is in operation at this site in line with transect 5, the most downstream transect. This reach has a smooth bedrock channel bottom with ledges that run parallel to flow. Parallel ledges are uncommon along most of the South Fork. Lynnwood also contains a particle riffle at transect 2 (table 6). Riverbend Pool, located upstream from the Town of Shenandoah (figs. 1, 7), is the next downstream

Table 5. Locations of river reaches studied during hydraulic data collection and fish habitat-suitability criteria development on the South Fork Shenandoah River, Virginia.

[Location information for the partial record station at each study reach. Reaches are presented in upstream to downstream order. DMS, degrees minutes seconds; NAD 83, North American Datum of 1983]

Station number	Reach name	Latitude DMS (NAD83)	Longitude DMS (NAD83)	Station name
01628500	Lynnwood	38 19′ 21″ N	78 45′ 18″ W	South Fork Shenandoah River near Lynnwood, Virginia
0162910630	Riverbend Pool	38 27′ 29″ N	78 38′ 00″ W	South Fork Shenandoah River above Naked Creek near Shenandoah, Virginia
01629510	Kauffman Mill	38 39′ 20″ N	78 32′ 30″ W	South Fork Shenandoah River below Route 211 near Hamburg, Virginia
01630555	Route 611[1]	38 44′ 57″ N	78 25′ 42″ W	South Fork Shenandoah River at Oak Hill, Virginia
01630600	Compton Pool[1]	38 47′ 01″ N	78 22′ 34″ W	South Fork Shenandoah River above Dry Run at Compton, Virginia
01630790	Thunderbird Farms	38 52′ 38″ N	78 15′ 26″ W	South Fork Shenandoah River below Gooney Run near Limeton, Virginia

[1]Only fish data were collected at these reaches.

Table 6.   Mesohabitat types represented by transects in the hydraulic data-collection reaches on the South Fork Shenandoah River, Virginia.

[Transects are numbered in upstream to downstream order, beginning with number 0 or 1]

Reach name	Transect	Habitat type	Reach name	Transect	Habitat type
Lynnwood	1	Run, bedrock	Kauffman Mill	0	Glide
	2	Riffle, particle		1	Riffle, particle
	3	Run, bedrock		2	Run, particle
	4	Run, bedrock		3	Run, bedrock
	5	Run, bedrock		4	Run, bedrock
Riverbend Pool	1	Pool, bedrock	Thunderbird Farms	1	Pool, bedrock
	2	Pool, bedrock		2	Pool, bedrock
	3	Pool, bedrock		3	Glide
				4	Riffle, bedrock

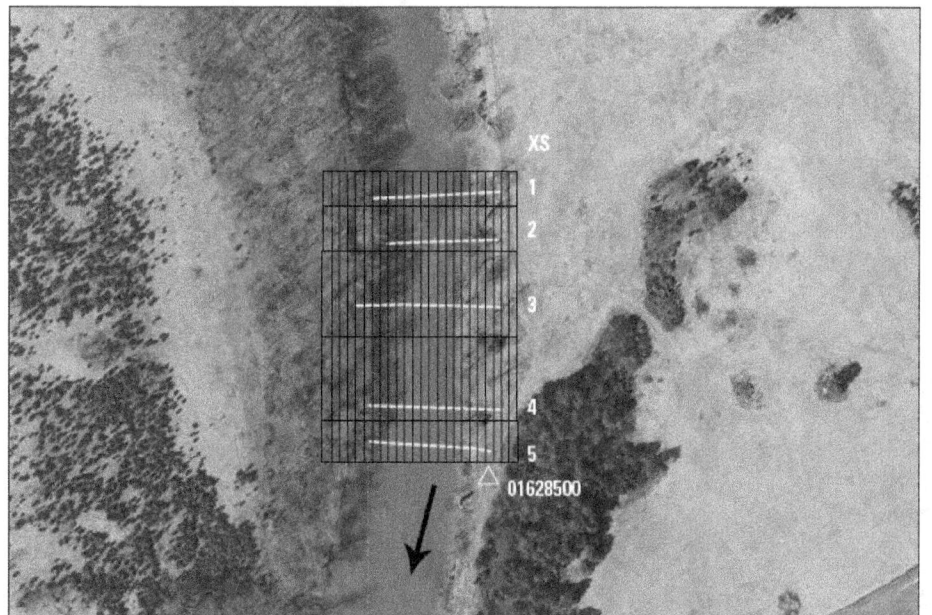

EXPLANATION

5 Transect location and number

☐ Model-grid habitat sampling cell

01628500 Streamflow-gaging station and number
▲

Model grid cells are 10 feet across.

Digital Orthophoto source: Virginia Geographic Information Network, 2007, VBMP Orthophotography—2006/2007 (VA State Plane North), 1:2,400 scale (1" = 200'), available online at *http://www.isp.virginia.gov/vbmporthophotography.shtml*

Figure 6.   Transect locations at Lynnwood on the South Fork of the Shenandoah River, Virginia. Locations of study sites are shown on figure 1.

reach. It is a natural pool with a control riffle downstream that is near the Shenandoah Dam Reservoir. Just upstream of Riverbend Pool is a high-gradient riffle at the point of a meander bend. The upstream transect at Riverbend Pool is a transitional transect, but slow and deep enough to be classified as bedrock pool. The two downstream cross sections (table 6) represent deeper pool habitats on the South Fork. These had slow velocities that averaged 0.15 foot per second (ft/s) during median low flows and less than 1.5 ft/s for the highest flows that were measured. The Kauffman Mill reach has the most diversity in habitat by having glide, particle riffle, particle run, and bedrock run transects. Kauffman Mill is located about 1 mi downstream from the streamflow-gaging station at Luray (figs. 1, 8), and about 4 mi upstream from the Luray Dam Reservoir. Transects 3 and 4 at the Kauffman Mill reach represent some of the last free-flowing water before the reservoir alters flow in the channel. The most downstream reach is Thunderbird Farms, located about 6 mi upstream from Front Royal (figs. 1, 9). Thunderbird Farms is mostly natural pool habitat (table 6) with a smooth bedrock bottom, which does not provide much cover or diversity in habitat for fish.

Standard PHABSIM data-collection procedures (Bovee, 1997) were used to collect channel and floodplain topographic information for each reach. One or two elevation benchmarks were set and surveyed using a GPS with submeter accuracy per reach as control points for a total station survey of transect markers and channel features. The GPS benchmarks for each reach allowed transect bed elevations and water-surface levels to be tied to a common elevation datum. Horizontal and vertical surveys of benchmarks, transect-marker elevations, and channel bed elevations were conducted with a surveying level or a total station, with an accuracy of 0.02 to 0.1 ft within a given reach. The surveys provided the distance between transects, water-surface slope, bed-elevation profiles, stage of zero-flow elevation, water depths, and benchmark locations and elevations. The primary benchmarks used when the transects were initially surveyed were maintained during the project and served as elevation control for WSL measurements during hydraulic data collection.

Jen Krstolic marking GPS waypoints on South Fork Shenandoah River

EXPLANATION

3 Transect location and number

☐ Model-grid habitat sampling cell

Model grid cells are 10 feet across.

Digital Orthophoto source: Virginia Geographic Information Network, 2007, VBMP Orthophotography—2006/2007 (VA State Plane North), 1:2,400 scale (1"= 200'), available online at *http://www.isp.virginia.gov/vbmporthophotography.shtml*

Figure 7.   Transect locations at Riverbend Pool on the South Fork of the Shenandoah River, Virginia. Locations of study sites are shown on figure 1.

Digital Orthophoto source: Virginia Geographic Information Network, 2007, VBMP Orthophotography—2006/2007
(VA State Plane North), 1:2,400 scale (1"= 200'), available online at *http://www.isp.virginia.gov/vbmporthophotography.shtml*

Figure 8.   Transect locations at Kauffman Mill on the South Fork of the Shenandoah River, Virginia.
Locations of study sites are shown on figure 1.

Digital Orthophoto source: Virginia Geographic Information Network, 2007, VBMP Orthophotography—2006/2007
(VA State Plane North), 1:2,400 scale (1"= 200'), available online at *http://www.isp.virginia.gov/vbmporthophotography.shtml*

Figure 9.   Transect locations at Thunderbird Farms on the South Fork of the Shenandoah River, Virginia.
Locations of study sites are shown on figure 1

Hydraulic Data-Collection Methods

Measurements of hydraulic data were made over a range of streamflows representative of the summer flow conditions at four study sites to provide calibration data for the RHABSIM physical habitat model. Measurements included WSL (or stage), water depth, water velocity, discharge, and substrate and cover characteristics relevant to fish habitat needs on the South Fork. Hydraulic measurements were made six or more times at all transects between May 2007 and August 2009 to represent summer low-flow, medium-flow, and high-flow conditions to develop a stage-discharge rating for each site. RHABSIM requires one discharge to represent the flow for a given reach for each day, even though the discharge measured at each transect may vary slightly. The modeling software refers to the representative reach discharge as the "best-estimate" discharge. Five best-estimate discharges that represent the widest flow range and most accurate stage-discharge relation for each site were selected and used as calibration discharges for the modeling phase of this research (table 7).

For each day of data collection, WSLs were measured with a surveying level to the nearest 0.001 ft at each transect before and after data collection. WSLs and observed discharges were checked each day in the field at Lynnwood and compared to the gage discharge and stage to ensure agreement of measured datasets. WSL differences between measured and gage stage for transect 5 ranged between 0.01 and 0.16 ft with a median value of 0.045 ft. Because of the difficulty of surveying stage in the field at Lynnwood, these numbers are likely the widest differences of all monitored study reaches. This check was helpful in assessing accuracy in WSL measurements at Lynnwood, but was not an option at the other study reaches where no gages were present.

A tagline was stretched across each transect, and water depths and velocities were recorded every 10 ft at the specified verticals for the reach. Depth and mean column velocity were measured with one of the following: a Flow Tracker

(SonTek YSI, Incorporated, 2006; calibrated to the nearest 0.01 ft/s), with a StreamPro (RD Instruments) Acoustic Doppler Current Profiler (ADCP) in "section-by-section" mode (calibrated to the nearest 0.01 ft/s); or a Price AA and Pygmy meter (calibrated to the nearest 0.01 ft/s). Depth and velocity measurements followed USGS procedures for discharge measurements (Buchanan and Somers, 1969), except that the spacing between velocity readings, or verticals, was constant. For all except the lowest discharges at a few sites, the ADCP "moving boat method" (Mueller and Wagner, 2009; Turnipseed and Sauer, 2010) was used to determine the best-estimate discharge in one transect per reach, because this is an approved method for calculating discharge (Mueller and Wagner, 2009). For the lowest discharges, Price AA or FlowTracker depth and velocity measurements from one transect per reach were used to calculate the best-estimate reach discharge. All transects were measured on the same day for a reach, but reaches were usually measured on different days during the same week.

Fish-Community Sampling and Microhabitat Observations

Fish habitat-use observations were conducted at USGS hydraulic data-collection reaches and at two additional sites (fig. 1) during June, July, August, and September of 2008. Flows during this timeframe were between the 10th and 75th percentile for each month, but most frequently at the 25th percentile flow (Ramey, 2009). Each study reach contained three to five transects, with each transect at a discrete mesohabitat type. Specific transects to be sampled for fish habitat use at each study reach were stratified by mesohabitat type and randomly selected in proportion to the relative abundance of each habitat type. A single study reach could contain more than one transect sampled. In total, eight transects at six study reaches were sampled using three sampling methodologies.

Data-Collection Methods

Fish habitat suitability criteria were developed with data from all three collection methods. The first method utilized a roving observer following sampling lanes as described in Bovee (1986) and Persinger (2003); the second method utilized a stationary observer in randomly selected sampling cells as described in Ramey (2009). Both methods used direct underwater observation (Goldstein, 1978; Thurow, 1994) to observe microhabitat use by fishes. Underwater visibility was considered adequate for sampling if an observer with mask and snorkel could see at least 3 ft to each side and from the water surface to the substrate. The third data-collection method was prepositioned electroshocking of areas sampled by the stationary observer (Ramey 2009).

Table 7. Best-estimate discharges used in the River Habitat Simulation model (RHABSIM) for each hydraulic data-collection reach on the South Fork Shenandoah River, Virginia.

Reach name	Calibration discharge, in cubic feet per second				
	1	2	3	4	5
Lynnwood	181	221	725	780	1,132
Riverbend Pool	271	380	554	962	1,187
Kauffman Mill	358	631	890	1,540	2,087
Thunderbird Farms	327	349	1,123	2,014	2,064

Electroshocking Crew—Clay and Julie Ramey, and Charlie Simmons (Virginia Department of Environmental Quality)

Observed fish were identified, counted, and size class recorded. In addition to the specified observation period while snorkeling, 10 rocks were flipped in each sampling unit (lanes or cells) to look for cryptic taxa including margined madtoms. A conscious effort was made not to count the same fish repeatedly, not to count fish that were obviously attracted to the observer, nor to count fish that were observed in microhabitats outside of the boundaries of sample cells or lanes.

Depth (measured to the nearest 0.1 ft) and mean column velocity (measured to the nearest 0.1 ft/s at 0.6 × depth) were measured with a FlowTracker (Sontek) on a graduated top-setting wading rod or with a StreamPro (RD Instruments) ADCP at the locations of the rover observer's fish markers and at the center of each of the 10 sample cells observed by the stationary observer.

Numerical codes for dominant and subdominant substrate size (table 8) based on a modified Wentworth scale (Bovee, 1986), cover (table 9), and embeddedness (see table 13 of Krstolic and others, 2006), were used so that substrate characterizations could be summarized in a single "channel index" (Krstolic and others, 2006). Where two or more cover types were present at a particular location, cover was characterized as "complex" in the channel index. Embeddedness was

Table 8. Substrate codes used to classify the dominant and subdominant substrate within fish study reaches and hydraulic data-collection reaches on the South Fork Shenandoah River, Virginia.

[Code modified from Krstolic and others, 2006. NA, not applicable; >, greater than; <, less than]

Code	Substrate category	Size, millimeters
1	Organic debris	NA
2	Silt	NA
3	Sand	< 2
4	Fine gravel	3 to 8
5	Small gravel	9 to 22
6	Large gravel	23 to 64
7	Small cobble	65 to 128
8	Large cobble	129 to 256
9	Small boulder	257 to 512
10	Large boulder	> 512
11	Bedrock	NA

Table 9. Codes used to classify the cover found around fish observations and within hydraulic data-collection reaches on the South Fork Shenandoah River, Virginia.

[Code modified from Krstolic and others, 2006]

Code	Description
1	No cover
2	Overhead limbs
3	Small woody debris
4	Large woody debris
5	Interstitial space
6	Boulder
7	Tilted bedrock
8	Submerged aquatic vegetation
9	Complex

Smallmouth bass (*Micropterus dolomieu*)

estimated visually as one of four categories: 0 to less than 25 percent, 25 to less than 50 percent, 50 to less than 75 percent, and 75 to 100 percent. Although channel index was evaluated for composite HSC rankings for each fish, what appeared to be the most important component of the channel index was the dominant substrate type. Therefore, for fish that had HSC defined, dominant substrate suitability was evaluated in the habitat suitability simulations, instead of channel index.

With few exceptions, fishes were identified to species. Spotfin and satinfin shiners (*Cyprinella spiloptera* and *C. analostana*) were indistinguishable from one another while swimming and were recorded as *Cyprinella* spp. Young-of-year of all species were assumed to be using specific habitat types; therefore, young-of-year were recorded as such without finer-scale distinction. Visually apparent life stages were recorded for juvenile, sub-adult, and adult when possible, and generally only for the species that attained the largest adult sizes.

Development and Testing of Fish Habitat Suitability Criteria

Habitat suitability criteria were evaluated only for taxa sampled on 30 or more events (following Maki-Petays and others, 2002), with the exception of adult smallmouth bass, which had an event sample size of only 18. Although 48 species or life stages were observed at least once during the study (Ramey, 2009), HSC were only evaluated for 9 species and life stages that had adequate sample size: sub-adult small-mouth bass and adult smallmouth bass (*Micropterus dolomieu*), juvenile redbreast sunfish, sub-adult redbreast sunfish, and adult redbreast sunfish (*Lepomis auritus*), satinfin or spotfin shiner (*Cyprinella* spp.), margined madtom (*Noturus insignis*), river chub (*Nocomis micropogon*), and young-of-year.

The habitat-use observations for depth, velocity, or channel index (substrate and cover) for each species were evaluated to determine ranges of *optimal, marginal, suitable,* and *unsuitable* habitat criteria (tables 10–12). *Optimal* habitats were defined as those within 25 percent of the median value, or the central 50 percent of the observed habitat parameter. *Marginal* habitats were represented by 15 percent greater than or less than the range of the central 50 percent of the observed habitat parameter. Habitats used by the central 80 percent of each taxa and life stage sampled (*optimal + marginal*) were

Table 10. Suitable range of depths for fish in the South Fork Shenandoah River, Virginia.

[Marginal, depths used by fish representing the central 80 percent of data; Optimal, depths used by fish representing the central 50 percent of data; n, number of samples]

Taxa/life stage	n (events)	Suitable range of depths, in feet			
		Lower		Upper	
		Marginal	Optimal	Optimal	Marginal
Sub-adult smallmouth bass	61	1.3	1.7	2.9	5.5
Smallmouth bass	[1]45	2.1	2.8	5.5	6.2
Juvenile redbreast sunfish	31	0.8	1.1	1.9	2.4
Sub-adult redbreast sunfish	31	1.3	1.8	3.6	4.4
Redbreast sunfish	30	0.9	1.6	3.5	4.5
Cyprinella spp.	61	0.9	1.1	1.8	2.4
Margined madtom	30	0.7	0.9	1.6	2.9
River chub	54	0.1	1.1	2.1	2.9
Young-of-year	37	0.9	1.1	2.0	3.7

[1]Used individual sample size for smallmouth bass (event n = 18).

Table 11. Suitable range of velocity for fish in the South Fork Shenandoah River, Virginia.

[Marginal, velocity used by fish representing the central 80 percent of data; Optimal, velocity used by fish representing the central 50 percent of data; n, number of samples]

Taxa/life stage	n (events)	Suitable range of velocity, in feet per second			
		Lower			Upper
		Marginal	Optimal		Marginal
Sub-adult smallmouth bass	61	0.13	0.26	1.21	1.77
Smallmouth bass	[1]45	0.05	0.17	0.69	1.17
Juvenile redbreast sunfish	31	0.01	0.16	0.90	1.28
Sub-adult redbreast sunfish	31	0.06	0.13	0.64	1.77
Redbreast sunfish	30	0.05	0.20	0.72	1.17
Cyprinella spp.	61	0.16	0.44	1.28	2.20
Margined madtom	30	0.08	0.64	1.43	2.96
River chub	54	0.14	0.58	1.64	2.35
Young-of-year	37	0.05	0.18	1.08	1.76

[1]Used individual sample size for smallmouth bass (event n = 18).

considered *suitable*, whereas *unsuitable* habitats were those with habitat parameters with ranges outside of those used by the central 80 percent of each taxa and life stage (following Persinger, 2003; Ramey, 2009).

To test whether the fish observations represented a preferential use of habitats, Student's T–tests were conducted for occupied and unoccupied habitats for each species with an adequate sample size. Student's T–test of occupied and unoccupied habitats showed that there were significant differences in depths where fish were present than depths where fish were not present for all species except young-of-year and sub-adult smallmouth bass ($\alpha = 0.05$) (fig. 10). Student's T–test of occupied and unoccupied habitats also showed that there were significant differences in velocities where fish were present than velocities where fish were not present for all species except young-of-year and sub-adult smallmouth bass and *Cyprinella* spp. ($\alpha = 0.05$) (fig. 10). These basic statistics provide insight to the fact that the fish were located in habitats preferentially and that their habitat selection was not likely to be random. Since young-of-year represent multiple species, it makes sense that they would not preferentially use a particular depth or velocity range, although the assumption had been that small fish would seek shelter in similar areas. Sub-adult smallmouth bass are generalist species, usually utilizing any available habitat to obtain their prey. In this study, however, separate data for sub-adult smallmouth bass and adult smallmouth bass were used in the habitat modeling, because when occupied habitat characteristics were evaluated between lifestages, both velocity and depth were significantly different

($\alpha = 0.05$). The mean depth or velocity values for occupied habitats for sub-adult redbreast sunfish and adult redbreast sunfish were not significantly different, so only the sub-adult redbreast sunfish were evaluated. The final HSC developed and tested in this study include sub-adult smallmouth bass and adult smallmouth bass, juvenile redbreast sunfish, sub-adult redbreast sunfish, and adult redbreast sunfish, *Cyprinella* spp., margined madtom, and river chub (app. 1).

Canoeing Suitability Criteria

Canoeing suitability criteria are based on the same depth and velocity ranges used for the North Fork and Shenandoah River mainstem studies (for criteria, see Zappia and Hayes, 1998; or Krstolic and others, 2006). The canoeing suitability criteria were created based on water depths considered to be adequate for passage (enough water to avoid stranding) across riffle areas. A minimum depth of 1 ft was considered marginal and given a suitability index value of 0.5. Depths greater than 2.5 ft were considered optimal and given a suitability index value of 1.0, indicating greater suitability for canoeing. Because excessive water velocities are considered hazardous for all but the most skilled paddlers, the velocity suitability index had an opposite pattern to depth. Velocity within the range of 0.5 to 2.5 ft/s were considered optimal and given an index value of 1.0, whereas velocities faster than 2.5 ft/s were considered marginal, and had decreasing index values. Velocities above 5 ft/s were considered unsuitable for canoeing. All substrates were considered suitable.

Table 12. Suitable range of channel index for fish in the South Fork Shenandoah River, Virginia.

[Marginal, channel index used by fish representing the central 80 percent of data; Optimal, channel index used by fish representing the central 50 percent of data; n, number of samples]

Taxa/life stage	n (events)	Suitable range of channel index			
		Lower			Upper
		Marginal	Optimal		Marginal
Sub-adult smallmouth bass	61	36.84	67.92	119.92	611.94
Smallmouth bass	[1]45	37.94	76.92	210.94	211.94
Juvenile redbreast sunfish	31	29.94	64.93	87.51	611.91
Sub-adult redbreast sunfish	31	28.94	67.51	117.91	210.94
Redbreast sunfish	30	33.94	63.53	117.91	711.91
Cyprinella spp.	61	56.91	67.52	117.91	611.91
Margined madtom	30	67.83	76.63	117.91	611.91
River chub	54	67.51	76.91	118.91	611.92
Young-of-year	37	28.94	37.94	116.91	611.91

[1]Used individual sample size for smallmouth bass (event n = 18).

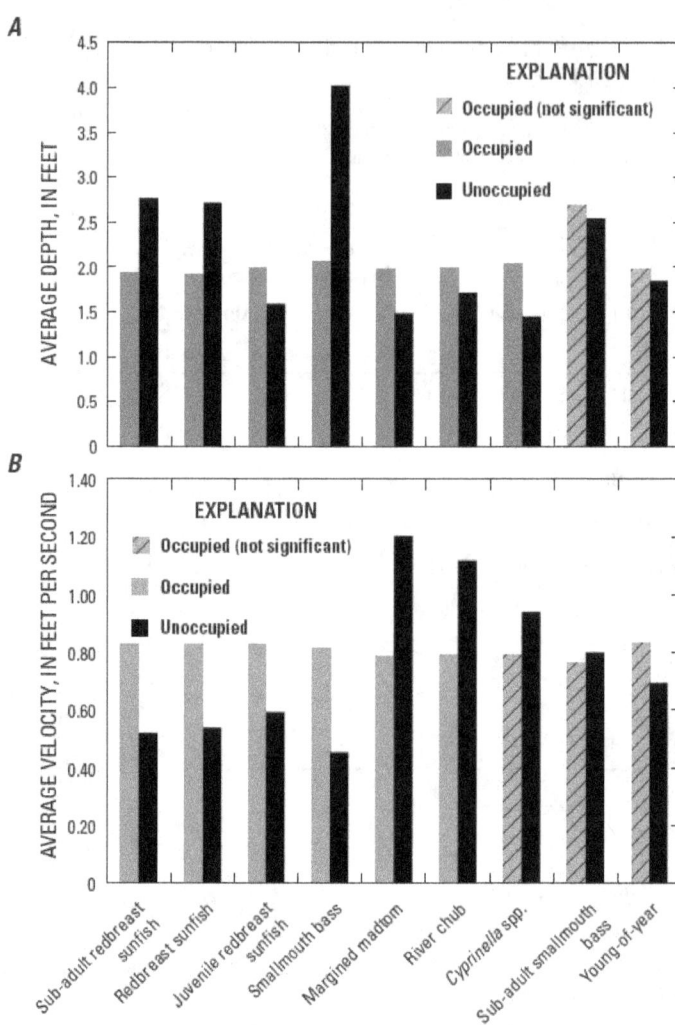

Figure 10. *A*, Average depth and *B*, average velocity data input to Student's T-test of occupied and unoccupied habitats for each species of the South Fork Shenandoah River, Virginia. Blue or green bars represent statistically significant differences between occupied and unoccupied habitats used by fish.

RHABSIM Modeling to Determine Fish Habitat Availability and Recreation Conditions

The program RHABSIM 3.0 for DOS and Windows (Thomas R. Payne and Associates, 1998) was used for calibration and simulation of flow and habitat. The RHABSIM modeling process includes two calibration phases and three simulation phases. Following the same methods used in Krstolic and others (2006), the WSL and velocity calibrations were completed first, followed by WSL, velocity, and habitat simulations. Calibration and simulation phases were performed separately for each reach, then in the upper reach habitat simulation results for two sites were combined.

Model Calibration

The RHABSIM model calibration uses the datasets collected during the hydraulic data-collection part of the study. Calibration involves inputting topographic information for each study reach, WSLs, velocities, and discharge

data for each hydraulic data-collection reach. The transect data are used to calculate stage-discharge ratings to enable simulation of depths and velocities for flows not measured during hydraulic data collection. Data input requirements for the South Fork were identical to the North Fork (Krstolic and others, 2006, p. 24). Because model calibration techniques were the same as those used for the North Fork project, only deviations of reach-specific details are presented in the sections that follow.

Water-Surface-Level Calibration

WSL models were selected for transects within each reach based on reach habitat conditions and hydraulic properties (table 13). As in Krstolic and others (2006) each model used the measured (observed) WSL, one discharge measurement per reach as the "best-estimate calibration discharge," and user-defined n-values or beta-values (hydraulic roughness parameters, as specified by the particular model). The hydraulic roughness parameters were used to adjust simulated conditions so that they accurately represent instream conditions by producing a simulated WSL that matched the measured value.

The model calibration was an iterative process, with new n-values or beta-values selected to minimize the difference between the observed and simulated WSL (Waddle, 2001). For sites with pool habitat where WSL did not vary greatly over the length of the reach (Thunderbird Farms and Riverbend Pool), the difference between observed and simulated WSL was less than or equal to 0.02 ft. For the two sites with more heterogeneous habitat and riffles in the central part of the reach (Kauffman Mill and Lynnwood), the difference between observed and simulated WSL ranged from 0.01 to 0.14 ft, depending on the simulation discharge and habitat at a given transect.

To assess accuracy of flows higher than calibration discharges, field data for WSL were compared to simulated WSL for selected high discharges. The Lynnwood simulation discharge of 3,840 ft^3/s was surveyed for WSL only, as the conditions were too high to collect data in the river. The simulated WSL were fairly consistent for transects 1 and 2 with the

surveyed WSL having a difference in range of 0 and 0.25 ft of the simulated WSL. The simulated WSL for transects 3, 4, and 5 were much lower than those surveyed in the field, with a WSL difference from 1.8 to 2 ft less than the simulated WSL. This indicates that the model is underpredicting depths for higher flows. The error in simulated WSL increases with discharge for calibration flows, and continues to increase as flows increase. The discharge of 3,840 ft^3/s was simulated to check the accuracy of the simulations, considering that this flow represents a 95th annual percentile flow (table 2), and is not likely to be important in the evaluation of flow thresholds for summer low-flow conditions.

For Kauffman Mill, a similar exercise was conducted with a dataset that was not used for calibration to compare simulated WSL to field surveyed WSL. The 2,087 ft^3/s field-surveyed WSL data were compared to simulated WSL, resulting in a difference of 0.003 to 0.39 ft. This discharge was much closer in magnitude to the highest calibration discharge, which likely accounts for the smaller differences in simulated and measured WSLs.

Table 13. Water-surface-level calibration methods and velocity calibration discharges used in the River Habitat Simulation model for each hydraulic data-collection reach and transect on the South Fork Shenandoah River, Virginia.

[WSL, water-surface level; ft^3/s, cubic feet per second; WSP, water-surface-profile method; MANSQ, Manning stage-discharge method; NA, not applicable. Transects are numbered in upstream to downstream order, beginning with number 0 or 1]

Reach	Transect	Habitat type	WSL calibration method[1]	WSL calibration discharge, ft^3/s	Beta, (MANSQ)	Manning's n (WSP)	Velocity calibration discharge, ft^3/s	Calculated discharge from simulated velocities, ft^3/s	Ratio difference: velocity adjustment factor	Percent difference
Lynnwood	1	Run, bedrock	WSP	780	NA	0.056	780	802	0.97	2.7
	2	Riffle, particle	WSP	780	NA	0.25	780	748	1.04	-4.3
	3	Run, bedrock	MANSQ	780	0.3993	NA	1,132	1,235	0.92	8.3
	4	Run, bedrock	MANSQ	780	0.5187	NA	780	812	0.96	3.9
	5	Run, bedrock	MANSQ	780	0.5136	NA	780	839	0.93	7.0
Riverbend Pool	1	Pool, bedrock	WSP	1,187	NA	0.0431	1,187	1,309	0.91	9.3
	2	Pool, bedrock	WSP	1,187	NA	0.13	1,187	797	1.49	-48.9
	3	Pool, bedrock	WSP	1,187	NA	0.13	1,187	1,238	0.96	4.1
Kauffman Mill	0	Glide	WSP	1,540	NA	0.0596	890	924	0.96	3.7
	1	Rifffle, particle	WSP	1,540	NA	0.035	358	928	0.39	61.4
	2	Run, particle	MANSQ	631	0.48	NA	890	877	1.01	-1.5
	3	Run, bedrock	MANSQ	631	0.62	NA	2,087	2,815	0.74	25.9
	4	Run, bedrock	MANSQ	631	0.64	NA	2,087	1,175	1.78	-77.6
Thunderbird Farms	1	Pool, bedrock	WSP	404	NA	0.05	404	410	0.99	1.5
	2	Pool, bedrock	WSP	404	NA	0.0503	1,123	1,238	0.91	9.3
	3	Glide	WSP	404	NA	0.1209	1,123	1,220	0.92	8.0
	4	Riffle, bedrock	WSP	404	NA	0.0275	1,123	1,213	0.93	7.4

[1]From Thomas R. Payne and Associates, 1998.

Although the literature would allow for extrapolation higher than the highest discharge measured, the accuracy of simulations declines greatly outside the bounds of the measured flows. For this investigation, the model application is related to low flows and conditions less than the 25th percentile flow. Should these models be used for other purposes, the underprediction of depths as flows increase outside the calibration discharge range should be considered.

When the WSL model calibration parameters were finalized and the WSLs had been simulated for the calibration discharges, the model was used to simulate WSLs for a set of 30 discharges representative of the flows within the 5th percentile to greater than the 95th percentile annual flow for each management section of the river (table 14). Simulation flows were spaced by about 100 ft^3/s to create regular intervals for simulation. Because the drainage areas associated with each of the hydraulic data-collection reach were within 1 percent of the drainage areas for the nearest gaging station, the model simulation flows were not corrected for drainage area differences between the hydraulic data-collection reach and the streamflow-gaging station.

Velocity Calibration

Velocity calibration procedures were very similar to those used with the North Fork models (Krstolic and others, 2006). The 1-velocity calibration method (Thomas R. Payne and Associates, 1998) was selected for all reaches and transects. For each transect, the velocity dataset that produced the least difference between the best-estimate discharge and model-calculated discharge was selected as the primary dataset to calibrate the velocity model (table 13). Cell by cell roughness values were adjusted to ensure a good match between the simulated velocity and measured velocity calibration dataset. Measured velocities for each model cell in the velocity calibration dataset were used as a template and adjusted based on the predicted depths from WSL simulations for higher or lower discharges. The model-calculated discharge for each transect was compared to best-estimate calibration discharge for the reach to obtain velocity adjustment factors (VAF) for each calibration discharge. After VAF were determined for calibration discharges, simple regressions were completed to incrementally increase the VAF for each simulation discharge. VAF were used to scale the velocity calibration dataset to simulate velocities for the 30 simulation flows. VAF were largest for transects with discharges that differ greatly from the best-estimate discharge, such as riffle transects.

Table 14.   Range of discharges used in the River Habitat Simulation model for simulations of water-surface levels, velocities, and habitats on the South Fork Shenandoah River, Virginia.

[Blue font values represent calibration flows]

Discharge, in cubic feet per second			
Lynnwood[1]	Riverbend Pool[2]	Kauffman Mill[3]	Thunderbird Farms[4]
72	108	124	130
122	181	174	179
181	238	224	228
221	271	262	290
265	380	358	327
337	424	380	349
360	481	470	404
460	554	520	450
544	600	570	557
604	690	631	599
725	747	681	698
780	804	731	831
880	861	769	897
980	918	890	948
1,050	962	996	1,123
1,132	1,032	1,140	1,213
1,200	1,187	1,290	1,312
1,300	1,327	1,440	1,412
1,400	1,469	1,540	1,490
1,500	1,584	1,700	1,760
1,600	1,698	1,800	1,908
1,900	1,790	2,089	2,064
2,100	1,869	2,390	2,360
2,400	2,040	2,500	2,444
2,600	2,212	2,770	2,742
2,800	2,554	3,070	3,160
3,000	2,725	3,250	3,734
3,400	2,897	3,550	4,230
3,840	3,000	3,850	4,650
4,200	3,068	No data	5,160

[1]The simulation discharges for Lynnwood represent a range between 0.40 times the lowest calibration flow and 3.7 times greater than the highest calibration flow.

[2]The simulation discharges for Riverbend Pool represent a range between 0.40 times the lowest calibration flow and 2.6 times greater than the highest calibration flow.

[3]The simulation discharges for Kauffman Mill represent a range between 0.35 times the lowest calibration flow and 2.5 times greater than the highest calibration flow.

[4]The simulation discharges for Thunderbird Farms represent a range between 0.40 times the lowest calibration flow and 2.5 times greater than the highest calibration flow.

Habitat Simulation and Development of Weighted Usable-Habitat Area Curves

Model cells input to RHABSIM for each study reach were centered on the verticals where depths and velocities were collected at 10-ft intervals, and substrate or cover measurements were made for 5 ft on either side of the center point. The length of model cells was varied based on habitat represented by the transect and the percentage of the reach upstream or downstream of the transect that contained the same habitat type. Transect weighting factors (app. 2) were used to determine model cell lengths, which are used to determine cell areas for available habitat. Figures 6–9 show variation in cell lengths among study sites.

The WSL and velocity simulations and the fish and canoeing HSC were input to the Habitat Simulation Model (HABSIM) of RHABSIM (Thomas R. Payne and Associates, 1998). HABSIM uses the HSC suitable ranges for water depths, water velocities, and dominant substrate to assign individual suitability ranks (on a scale from 0.0 to 1.0) for depth, velocity, and substrate in each model cell. Multiplicative aggregation (Waddle, 2001) was used to calculate the composite suitability rank for each cell, which also produced a composite score between 0.0 and 1.0. The area of all suitable habitat cells within a reach was summed for a total weighted usable-habitat area (WUA). The process was repeated for each species or lifestage of fish and canoeing over 30 simulation flows, and a functional relation between habitat and discharge was defined and expressed in the form of WUA curves.

For recreation, particularly canoeing, adequate water depth to avoid scraping bottom is a major consideration. Therefore, habitat simulations for canoeing had additional restrictions placed on depth to include only cells that are 1-ft deep or greater. No restrictions on velocity suitability, other than the HSC suitability ranks, were implemented.

As was done in the North Fork study, the South Fork Shenandoah River basin study reaches were placed in upper, middle, and lower sections that are associated with the streamflow-gaging stations (Lynnwood, Luray, and Front Royal) near the downstream end of each section. Unlike the North Fork where the discharge doubles between streamflow-gaging stations, the median annual streamflow only increases by 224 ft³/s (145 Mgal/d) between Lynnwood and Luray, and increases by 120 ft³/s (78 Mgal/d) between Luray and Front Royal. The largest amount of water withdrawals occur in the Lynnwood section, which has the least amount of water availability, so two hydraulic study reaches were placed in this section. The other two downstream sections each have one study reach. Transects in each reach were weighted (app. 2) to represent the total percentage of habitat available in that section of the river based on data from table 4.

Habitat-Discharge Relations for Streamflow-Gaging Stations on the South Fork

Lynnwood Ecological Habitat

For this investigation, the Lynnwood streamflow-gaging station and hydraulic data-collection reaches in this section represent discharge in the reach between the confluence of the North, Middle, and South Rivers up to the Shenandoah Dam. Lynnwood and Riverbend Pool study reaches were located in this section. The Lynnwood reach contains run and riffle habitats, whereas the Riverbend Pool contains only pool habitat. A RHABSIM model was calibrated for WSL and velocities collected from field data and evaluated against fish HSC (tables 10–12; app. 2) for the seven species or lifestages of fish discussed earlier in this document. The amount of available usable habitat, weighted for the percentage of each type of habitat present in this section of the river to generate WUA, was calculated for a range of streamflows from 72 to 4,200 ft³/s for the Lynnwood reach and 108 to 3,068 ft³/s for Riverbend Pool (table 14). The WUA for each reach and the combined upper section of river is shown in tables 15–17, and figs. 11–13.

To illustrate the amount of WUA commonly expected for each fish during the low-flow period, the JAS normal range of flows (265 to 544 ft³/s), the 10th percentile flow (203 ft³/s) for JAS flows, the 5th percentile flow (178 ft³/s) for JAS flows, and the annual 7Q10 statistic (151.0 ft³/s) were plotted over each set of WUA curves (figs. 11–13). Riverbend Pool and Lynnwood individual reach model result figures are shown (figs. 12, 13) to illustrate how different habitat types (a pool, a riffle or run, respectively) produced varying amounts of WUA for each species. However, this discussion involves the combined curves (Riverbend Pool + Lynnwood) for the upper section so that pools, riffles, and runs are all represented. The normal range of flows for JAS included the maximum WUA for sub-adult redbreast sunfish and sub-adult smallmouth bass, whereas WUA curves increased for *Cyprinella* spp., river chub, margined madtom, and juvenile redbreast sunfish as flows decreased within the normal range of flows for JAS. Lower flows provided habitat for smaller, riffle-dwelling fishes, as indicated by the WUA curve peaks which occurred at 181 ft³/s for river chub and at 221 ft³/s for *Cyprinella* spp. and margined madtom. The maximum WUA for juvenile redbreast sunfish occurred at flows lower than the 5th percentile flow. By the time flows reached the 5th percentile for JAS flow, habitat availability was declining for all species except juvenile redbreast sunfish.

Adult smallmouth bass habitat availability was lower than that for any other species in the combined reaches (fig. 11) modeled for the upper section of the river, but was relatively abundant in the Riverbend Pool reach (fig. 13). The WUA in the Riverbend Pool reach illustrates adult smallmouth bass dependence on deeper pool habitats, but also shows the upper boundary of depths that are "too deep" based on observations (or lack of fish presence). The rest of the species studied did not exhibit a preference for deep-water habitats found at Riverbend Pool and would likely be found only at the edges.

Table 15.   Weighted usable-habitat area, in square feet per 1,000 feet of stream, for the upper section, including the Lynnwood study reach and the Riverbend Pool study reach on the South Fork Shenandoah River, Virginia.

[Mgal/d, million gallons per day; ft³/s, cubic feet per second; ND, no data simulated for this flow]

| Simulated discharge, Mgal/d | Simulated discharge, ft³/s | Ecological habitat | | | | | | | Recreational habitat |
| | | Fish species | | | | | | | |
		Sub-adult smallmouth bass	Adult smallmouth bass	Juvenile redbreast sunfish	Sub-adult redbreast sunfish	*Cyprinella* spp.	Margined madtom	River chub	Canoeing
46.5	72	17,427	6,837	50,640	33,645	23,682	22,613	50,936	38,107
78.8	122	32,815	11,507	55,812	57,955	39,982	30,712	68,261	74,287
117.0	181	38,663	19,562	50,261	54,144	42,725	40,795	95,909	100,214
142.8	221	40,852	18,718	47,006	52,869	43,374	42,614	93,934	114,191
217.8	337	45,906	19,722	26,672	62,867	31,985	38,639	89,171	155,042
232.7	360	45,640	21,350	24,061	64,635	31,002	39,382	84,704	168,022
297.3	460	33,355	25,210	15,551	59,452	23,284	32,178	73,694	195,838
351.6	544	29,385	25,586	11,788	57,373	18,129	30,376	62,465	206,560
390.3	604	26,542	24,470	11,387	51,576	13,829	26,254	51,513	218,549
468.5	725	19,037	24,414	10,138	42,112	12,269	21,859	34,829	227,526
504.1	780	13,806	23,102	10,259	33,872	9,828	20,644	29,469	234,868
568.7	880	11,365	23,463	8,973	28,631	7,718	17,162	26,014	234,014
633.3	980	9,469	26,332	8,387	26,610	7,073	16,275	21,347	233,035
678.6	1050	9,836	24,833	9,489	25,447	6,721	15,431	18,407	236,647
731.6	1132	11,318	26,089	10,321	27,507	5,637	14,643	16,277	237,306
775.5	1200	11,931	24,606	9,670	29,071	4,727	13,263	12,077	235,581
840.2	1300	8,853	22,034	7,535	25,780	3,377	11,824	11,056	228,542
904.8	1400	8,027	21,093	7,036	24,754	3,718	11,200	9,945	220,004
969.4	1500	7,434	20,181	7,048	23,849	3,738	8,744	10,093	213,028
1,034.0	1600	8,202	19,280	6,861	23,264	4,354	6,460	9,863	207,297
1,227.9	1900	6,875	21,323	5,376	19,999	2,900	3,845	8,111	201,796
1,357.2	2100	6,693	19,947	5,191	17,470	2,784	3,930	7,816	196,307
1,551.1	2400	7,066	20,686	5,301	16,716	3,027	4,319	6,255	185,476
1,680.3	2600	7,607	21,790	4,518	18,488	1,903	3,540	6,263	176,471
1,809.6	2800	3,815	3,304	2,076	7,203	1,903	3,173	5,313	ND
1,938.8	3000	3,834	3,304	2,203	6,945	1,168	3,556	4,224	ND
2,197.3	3400	2,904	1,124	1,457	6,872	671	3,637	3,289	ND
2,481.7	3840	3,144	2,828	3,975	8,233	3,006	6,099	6,402	ND
2,714.3	4200	3,634	3,211	3,669	8,331	3,008	5,529	5,733	ND

Table 16.   Weighted usable-habitat area, in square feet per 1,000 feet of stream, for the Riverbend Pool study reach on the South Fork Shenandoah River, Virginia.

[Mgal/d, million gallons per day; ft³/s, cubic feet per second]

Simulated discharge, Mgal/d	Simulated discharge, ft³/s	Ecological habitat							Recreational habitat
		Fish species							Canoeing
		Sub-adult smallmouth bass	Adult smallmouth bass	Juvenile redbreast sunfish	Sub-adult redbreast sunfish	*Cyprinella* spp.[1]	Margined madtom[1]	River chub[1]	
117	181	1,254	8,751	4,255	9,190	0	0	0	1,164
154	238	1,376	10,762	3,806	8,999	0	0	0	9,191
175	271	2,180	11,658	4,953	10,258	0	0	0	16,722
246	380	3,751	12,543	4,644	14,836	0	0	0	44,255
274	424	3,848	15,265	4,629	15,845	0	0	0	55,215
311	481	4,591	18,052	4,014	17,525	0	0	0	65,464
358	554	4,340	21,956	3,645	16,692	0	0	0	75,392
388	600	4,239	22,334	3,528	16,483	0	0	0	82,004
446	690	5,198	21,580	3,583	15,957	0	0	0	93,036
483	747	5,175	22,410	2,961	15,826	0	0	0	98,389
520	804	4,591	22,969	2,661	17,116	0	0	0	104,146
557	861	4,776	21,662	2,551	15,911	0	195	0	109,755
594	918	4,694	21,657	2,888	16,112	0	402	0	114,347
622	962	4,587	21,873	3,357	16,209	0	414	0	117,736
667	1,032	4,177	24,364	2,147	14,974	0	414	0	121,450
768	1,187	4,171	22,477	2,210	13,807	0	0	0	129,461
858	1,327	4,249	22,477	2,199	15,349	0	0	0	136,430
950	1,469	5,828	21,651	1,959	17,631	0	0	0	140,973
1,024	1,584	4,970	19,144	1,843	16,454	0	0	0	143,599
1,098	1,698	4,378	18,203	1,328	15,041	0	194	0	145,980
1,158	1,790	3,423	17,292	1,174	14,552	0	371	0	147,785
1,209	1,869	3,315	17,666	1,183	14,295	0	420	0	149,447
1,319	2,040	3,315	19,955	1,296	12,534	0	420	0	152,250
1,431	2,212	3,240	18,950	1,693	10,729	0	285	0	154,008
1,652	2,554	3,315	17,473	2,173	9,843	0	0	0	152,099
1,762	2,725	3,384	17,473	2,845	10,247	0	0	0	147,072
1,874	2,897	4,202	18,486	2,372	11,660	0	0	0	141,527
1,940	3,000	4,397	18,320	2,262	11,398	0	0	0	138,950
1,984	3,068	4,619	18,320	2,267	10,127	0	0	0	137,305

[1]Shallow-water species habitat was limited by water depths that were too deep even at the lowest flows simulated.

Table 17.   Weighted usable-habitat area, in square feet per 1,000 feet of stream, for the Lynwood study reach on the South Fork Shenandoah River, Virginia.

[Mgal/d, million gallons per day; ft³/s, cubic feet per second]

Simulated discharge, Mgal/d	Simulated discharge, ft³/s	Ecological habitat							Recreational habitat
		Fish species							Canoeing
		Sub-adult smallmouth bass	Adult smallmouth bass	Juvenile redbreast sunfish	Sub-adult redbreast sunfish	Cyprinella spp.	Margined madtom	River chub	
79	122	31,562	2,756	51,557	48,765	39,982	30,712	68,261	73,124
117	181	37,288	8,800	46,455	45,144	42,725	40,795	95,909	91,023
143	221	38,672	7,060	42,053	42,611	43,374	42,614	93,934	97,469
171	265	42,102	8,896	34,913	45,687	39,481	41,203	93,079	103,297
218	337	42,156	7,179	22,027	48,031	31,985	38,639	89,171	110,787
233	360	41,792	6,085	19,433	48,790	31,002	39,382	84,704	112,807
297	460	29,014	3,253	11,906	42,760	23,284	32,178	73,694	120,446
352	544	25,146	3,252	8,259	40,889	18,129	30,376	62,465	124,556
390	604	21,344	2,890	7,803	35,618	13,829	26,254	51,513	125,513
469	725	14,446	1,445	7,476	24,996	12,269	21,859	34,829	123,380
504	780	9,111	1,445	7,371	17,760	9,828	20,241	29,469	120,521
569	880	6,778	1,590	5,616	12,422	7,718	16,748	26,014	116,279
633	980	5,292	1,968	6,240	11,636	7,073	15,862	21,347	111,585
679	1050	5,665	2,356	7,279	11,640	6,721	15,431	18,407	107,186
732	1132	7,069	3,612	8,122	12,157	5,637	14,643	16,277	100,876
776	1200	6,103	2,955	7,711	11,440	4,727	13,263	12,077	94,609
840	1300	3,883	2,890	5,693	9,326	3,377	11,824	11,056	84,942
905	1400	3,649	2,890	5,709	9,713	3,718	11,006	9,945	74,024
969	1500	4,011	2,890	5,874	9,297	3,738	8,372	10,093	65,244
1,034	1600	4,888	1,613	5,678	8,969	4,354	6,040	9,863	57,850
1,228	1900	3,635	2,373	3,683	9,270	2,900	3,560	8,111	47,788
1,357	2100	3,378	2,474	3,018	7,627	2,784	3,930	7,816	44,208
1,551	2400	3,682	3,213	2,456	6,469	3,027	4,319	6,255	38,404
1,680	2600	3,406	3,304	2,146	6,828	1,903	3,540	6,263	34,944
1,810	2800	3,815	3,304	2,076	7,203	1,903	3,173	5,313	32,174
1,939	3000	3,834	3,304	2,203	6,945	1,168	3,556	4,224	30,199
2,197	3400	2,904	1,124	1,457	6,872	671	3,637	3,289	27,080
2,482	3840	3,144	2,828	3,975	8,233	3,006	6,099	6,402	23,447
2,714	4200	3,634	3,211	3,669	8,331	3,008	5,529	5,733	20,093

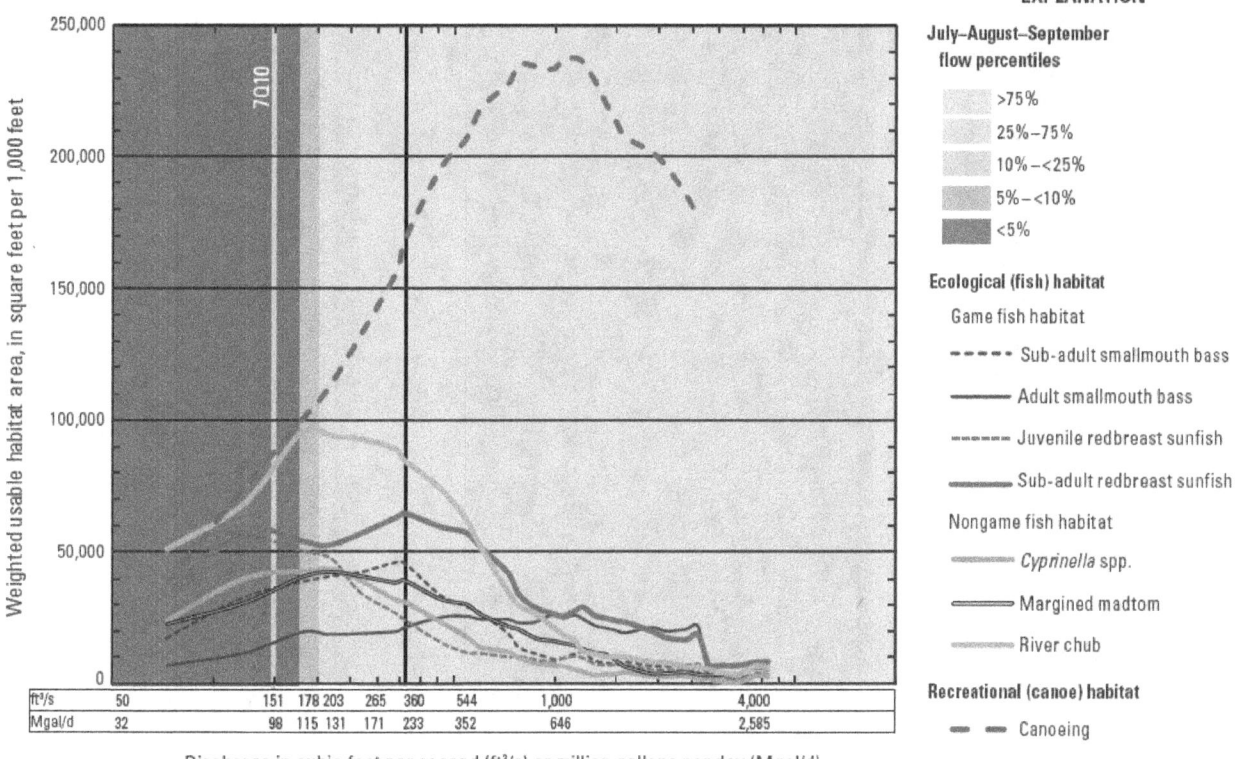

Discharge in cubic feet per second (ft³/s) or million gallons per day (Mgal/d)

Figure 11.   Weighted usable-habitat area of ecological and recreational habitat combined for the Lynnwood and Riverbend Pool study reaches on the South Fork of the Shenandoah River, Virginia. Flow percentiles are based on data from the Lynnwood streamflow-gaging station (01628500) from 1930 to 2008 for streamflows during the months of July, August, and September. These statistics represent the expected range of flows, based on the historic streamflow record.

Bedrock riffle, South Fork Shenandoah River

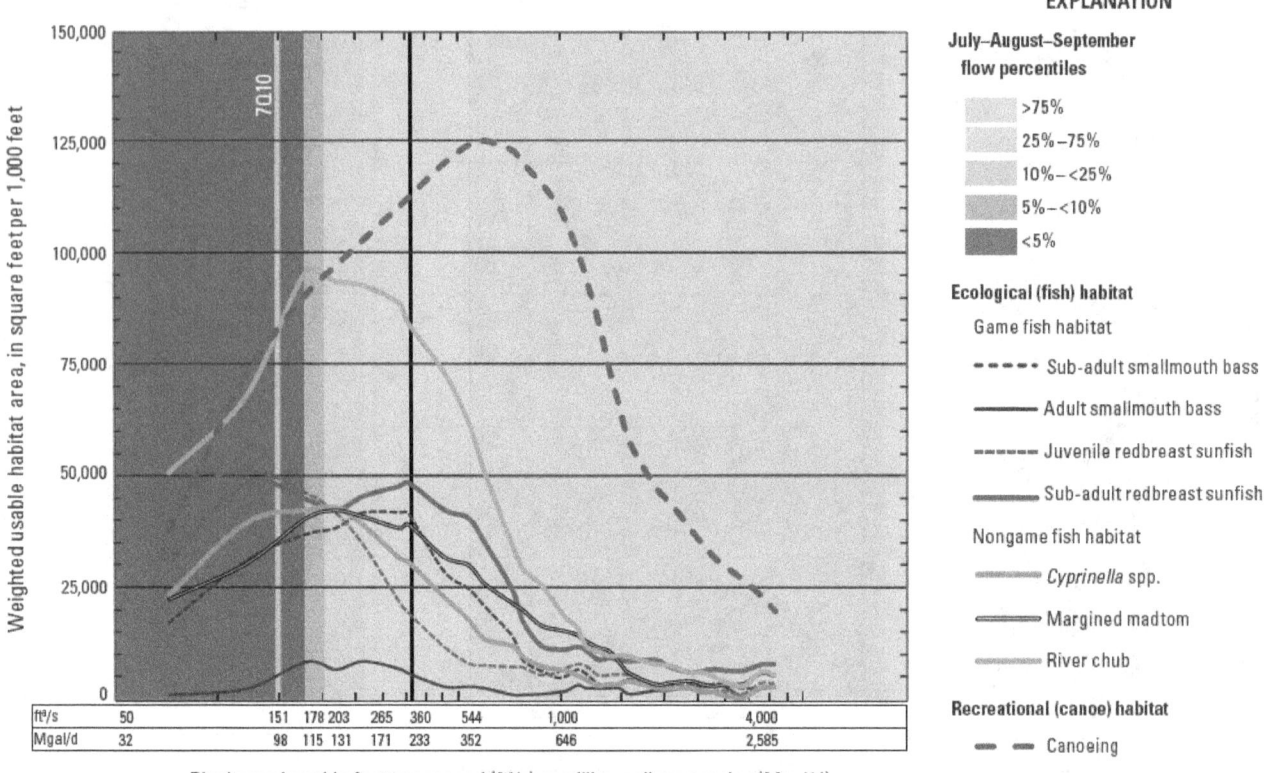

Figure 12. Weighted usable-habitat area of ecological and recreational habitat at the Lynnwood study reach on the South Fork of the Shenandoah River, Virginia. Flow percentiles are based on data from the Lynnwood streamflow-gaging station (01628500) from 1930 to 2008 for streamflows during the months of July, August, and September. These statistics represent the expected range of flows, based on the historic streamflow record.

Downstream view, South Fork Shenandoahh River near Lynnwood

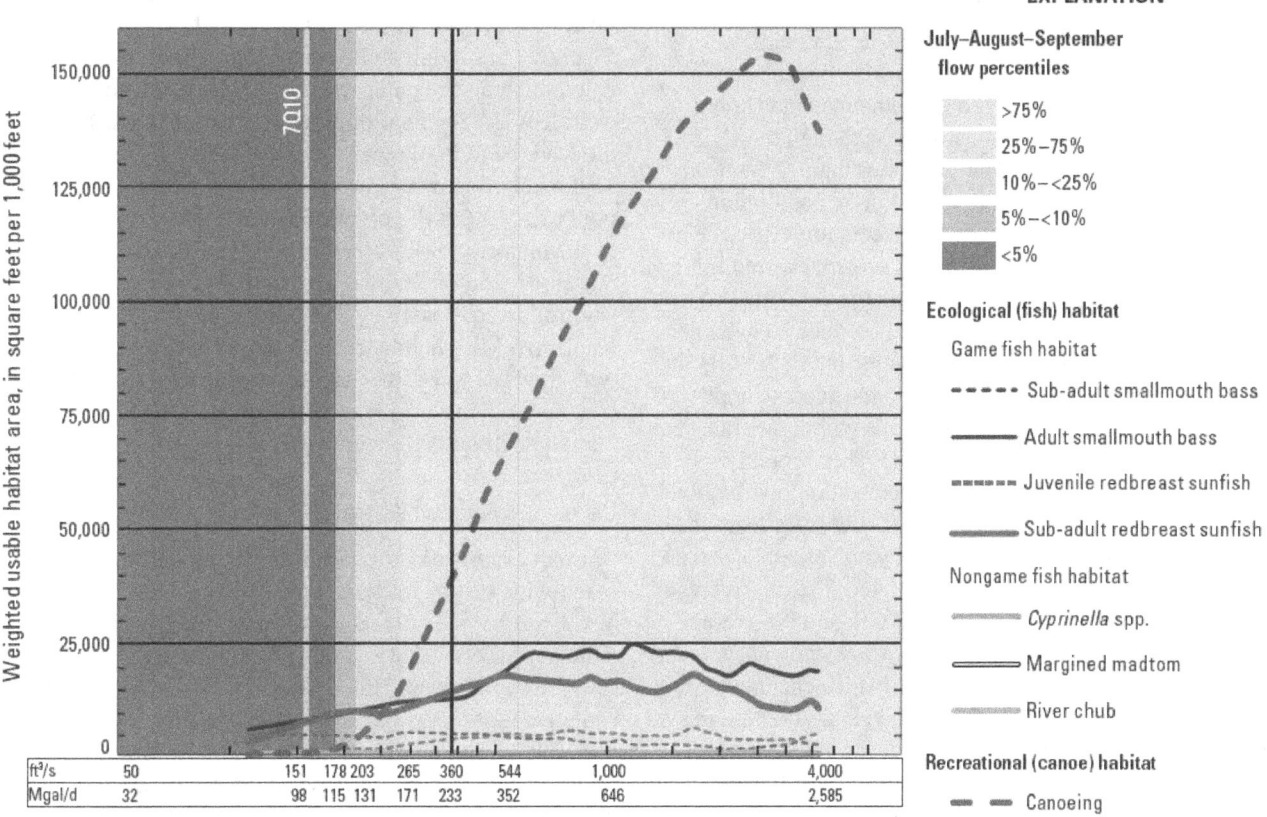

Figure 13.   Weighted usable-habitat area of ecological and recreational habitat at the Riverbend Pool study reach on the South Fork of the Shenandoah River, Virginia. Simulation results had no available habitat for *cyprinella* spp., margined madtom, or river chub at this site. Flow percentiles are based on data from the Lynnwood streamflow-gaging station (01628500) from 1930 to 2008 for streamflows during the months of July, August, and September. These statistics represent the expected range of flows, based on the historic streamflow record.

Dennis Adams making an ADCP measurement along the
South Fork Shenandoah River

Canoeing through the Lynnwood Section

Although two study reaches are included in the Lynnwood section, only the Lynnwood study reach has riffle habitat. Riverbend Pool is all pool habitat and should not present any difficulties for canoeing, although the slow velocity range (0.2 to 0.5 ft/s for flows less than 1,050 ft^3/s) suggest that the paddler may have to do more paddling in this section. The Lynnwood study reach contains one riffle at transect 2, which was used to identify flows that would limit depths suitable for canoe passage. Discharge equal to 360 ft^3/s represents the lowest discharge that will produce an average depth of 1 ft for the transect, a maximum depth of 2.37 ft, and an average velocity of 2.1 ft/s. Although the average depth is equal to 1 ft, almost half of the study cells within the transect will not meet this requirement (fig. 14A). These conditions are what can be expected for the 50th percentile flow for JAS (360 ft^3/s, table 2). A discharge of 460 ft^3/s ensures that the majority of the cells across the channel width are greater than or equal to 1-ft deep. For a discharge of 460 ft^3/s, the average depth is 1.2 ft, the maximum depth is 2.6 ft, and the average velocity is 2.4 ft/s (fig. 14B). The Lynnwood study reach has bedrock ledges that run parallel to flow, which channelize water and create focused areas of faster velocity. Where this form of bedrock occurs along transect 3, the average velocities reach 4.1 ft/s at 2,400 ft^3/s and 5.1 ft/s at 3,400 ft^3/s. The Lynnwood study reach WUA curves for canoeing (fig. 12) show that the maximum canoeing habitat occurs with a discharge of 604 ft^3/s, and a decline in canoeing habitat occurs at flows greater than 604 ft^3/s.

Luray Ecological Habitat

For this investigation, the Luray streamflow-gaging station and Kauffman Mill hydraulic data-collection reach represent discharge and habitat for the stretch of river from the Shenandoah Dam to the Luray Dam. As mentioned previously, Kauffman Mill contains glide, run, and riffle habitats. A RHABSIM model was calibrated for water-surface levels and velocities that were collected from field data and evaluated against HSC (tables 10–12; app. 1) for the seven species or lifestages of fish discussed earlier in this document. The amount of available usable habitat, weighted for the percentage of each type of habitat present in the river, WUA, was calculated for a range of streamflows from 124 to 3,850 ft^3/s (table 14). The WUA for Kauffman Mill and the middle section of the river is shown in table 18 and figure 15.

To illustrate the amount of WUA commonly expected for each fish during the low-flow period, the JAS normal range of flows (380 to 769 ft^3/s), the 10th percentile flow (310 ft^3/s) for JAS flows, the 5th percentile flow (262 ft^3/s) for JAS flows, and the annual 7Q10 statistic (225.0 ft^3/s) were plotted over each set of WUA curves (fig. 15). The normal range of flows for JAS includes the maximum WUA for all fish except juvenile and sub-adult redbreast sunfish. For these species the maximum WUA occurs close to the 25th percentile flow, and thereafter, habitat availability

declines as flows decline. Maximum WUA for sub-adult and juvenile redbreast sunfish occurs with flows lower than the 5th percentile. Adult smallmouth bass habitat availability is less than all the other species in this reach; however, the overall WUA for smallmouth bass is almost double that of the Riverbend Pool reach. The low WUA in the Kauffman Mill reach illustrates smallmouth bass dependence on deep pool habitats (on the order of 5 to 6 ft deep), but not as deep as the majority of Riverbend Pool (15 ft). River chub and margined madtom habitat availability is maximized at this site, followed closely by sub-adult smallmouth bass. At Kauffman Mill, habitat availability seems to be maintained with flows as low as the 10th percentile flow (310 ft^3/s) (fig. 15). When flows reach the annual 7Q10 flow statistic, habitat declines are observed for all species.

Canoeing through the Luray Section

An examination of each transect, as well as the WUA reach-wide results for Kauffman Mill, help to put the canoeing WUA results into context. Kauffman Mill has a high-gradient riffle at transect 1 that is a limiting feature for paddlers during low-flow conditions. This riffle is considered to be representative of larger riffles in the Luray section. Flows equal to 520 ft^3/s provide an average depth of 1.3 ft, a maximum depth of 2.17 ft, and an average velocity of 1.3 ft/s for the riffle at transect 1. Flows equal to 262 ft^3/s (the 5th percentile flow for JAS) provide adequate depths at only a few sections along transect 1. To ensure that transect 1 is passable along the majority of the channel width, paddlers may want to select days when discharge is equal to or greater than 520 ft^3/s. For a flow of 520 ft^3/s, the combined depth and velocity suitability criteria are met for 75 percent of the reach area (fig. 16A). The other transects at Kauffman Mill are run or glide habitats and should not create difficulties for paddlers. These modeling results are close to the minimum discharge suggested by local outfitter organizations who offer river trips between Luray and Front Royal. One company suggests that 404 ft^3/s at the Luray gage is very low, and that ideal paddling conditions are 830 to 3,070 ft^3/s (Downriver Canoe Co., 2011). The RHABSIM modeling results suggest that the maximum canoeing habitat occurs at 890 ft^3/s (table 18, figs. 15–16B). Model results and outfitters agree that flows near 800 ft^3/s represent suitable canoeing conditions for the Luray section of the South Fork.

Front Royal Ecological Habitat

For this investigation the Front Royal streamflow-gaging station and Thunderbird Farms hydraulic data-collection reach measurements are used to represent discharge in the reach between Luray to the gage at Front Royal. As mentioned previously, Thunderbird Farms contains pool, glide, and riffle habitats. A RHABSIM model was calibrated for water-surface levels and velocities collected from field data and evaluated against HSC (tables 10–12; app. 1) for the seven species or lifestages of fish discussed earlier in this document. The amount of available usable habitat, weighted for

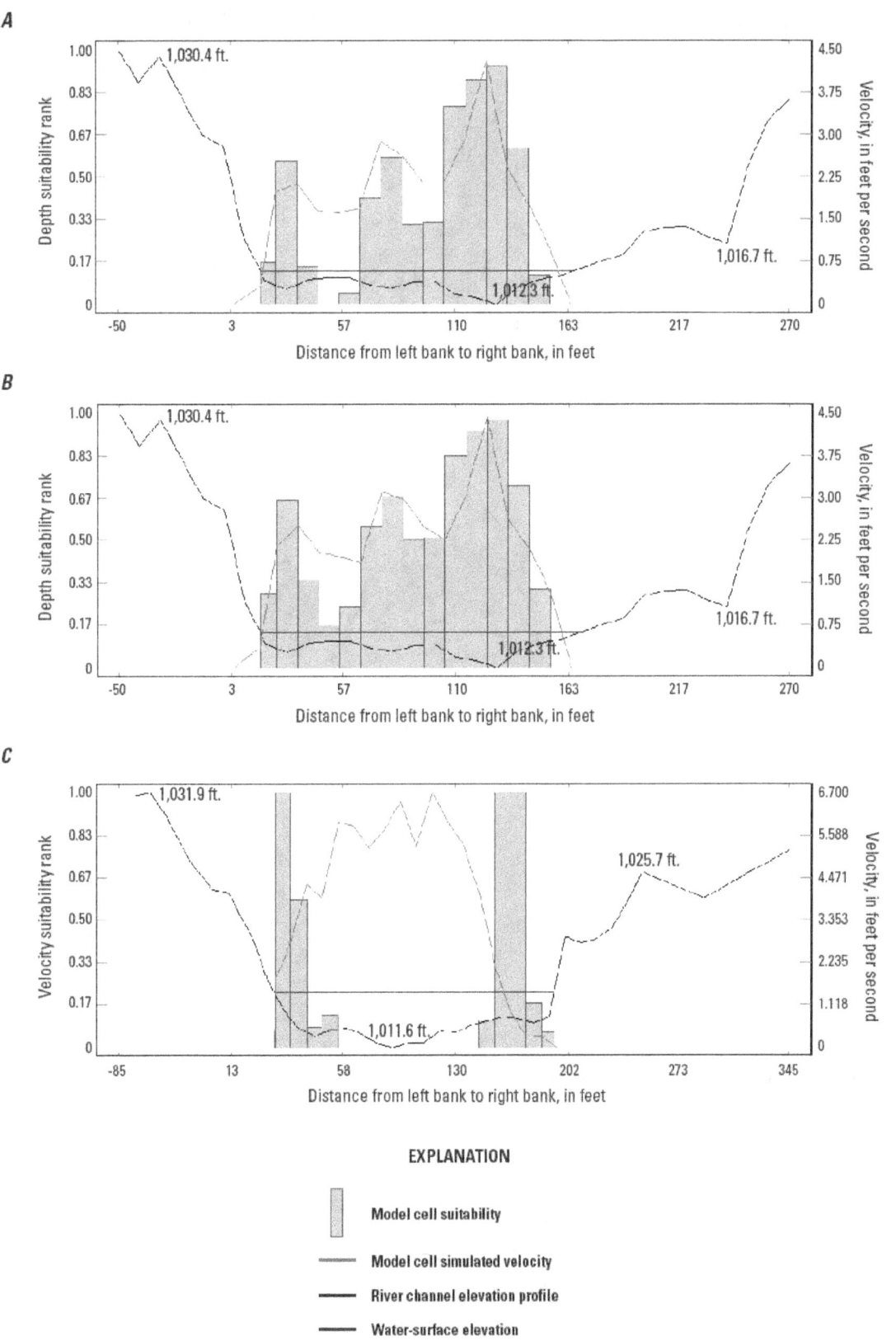

Figure 14.   Canoeing suitability for selected transects at the Lynnwood study reach on the South Fork of the Shenandoah River, Virginia. *A*, depth suitability and simulated velocity for riffle habitat at transect 2 associated with the simulated discharge equal to 360 cubic feet per second (ft³/s); *B*, depth suitability and simulated velocity for riffle habitat at transect 2 associated with the simulated discharge equal to 460 ft³/s; and *C*, velocity suitability and simulated velocity for run habitat at transect 3 associated with simulated discharge equal to 2,400 ft³/s.

Table 18.   Weighted usable-habitat area, in square feet per 1,000 feet of stream, for the Kauffman Mill study reach on the South Fork Shenandoah River, Virginia.

[Mgal/d, million gallons per day; ft³/s, cubic feet per second]

Simulated discharge, Mgal/d	Simulated discharge, ft³/s	Ecological habitat							Recreational habitat
		Fish species							
		Sub-adult smallmouth bass	Adult smallmouth bass	Juvenile redbreast sunfish	Sub-adult redbreast sunfish	*Cyprinella* spp.	Margined madtom	River chub	Canoeing
112	174	75,455	40,168	86,230	106,770	64,890	66,794	90,985	111,873
145	224	83,507	45,167	84,438	105,670	71,211	81,842	113,923	136,749
169	262	88,481	42,553	80,758	96,426	73,329	95,841	127,891	148,590
231	358	93,541	44,804	65,469	85,830	70,273	103,739	136,132	166,599
246	380	96,930	41,731	63,593	83,898	72,728	105,912	138,240	169,396
304	470	100,278	39,626	43,813	88,399	63,416	101,780	135,104	178,946
336	520	93,898	35,945	41,420	88,559	62,671	98,254	128,742	183,288
368	570	85,738	31,954	34,826	84,569	56,807	90,372	123,595	186,812
408	631	76,707	24,606	31,257	83,220	54,141	84,460	116,461	190,616
472	731	66,784	20,345	21,063	79,085	45,554	74,339	100,662	194,917
497	769	62,950	19,270	19,078	78,035	41,395	70,564	96,683	196,199
575	890	48,991	14,366	16,042	63,520	32,813	60,379	76,787	197,442
644	996	40,341	13,421	12,744	51,244	23,442	52,125	65,357	195,648
737	1,140	32,099	13,436	10,199	41,465	19,405	42,260	50,591	190,758
834	1,290	25,446	9,982	9,999	34,463	16,629	34,222	38,840	183,541
931	1,440	22,542	9,958	8,827	28,561	13,184	29,446	31,080	171,779
995	1,540	18,562	8,128	8,882	22,126	10,759	27,234	25,442	159,930
1,099	1,700	16,726	6,570	9,258	19,610	5,870	23,974	22,572	141,571
1,163	1,800	15,627	6,858	9,656	18,592	5,072	21,949	21,817	131,761
1,350	2,089	14,261	7,157	10,321	18,736	5,808	19,474	15,835	108,796
1,480	2,290	12,531	8,045	10,135	18,209	4,437	17,456	13,246	97,229
1,616	2,500	12,401	8,047	8,645	17,579	4,431	14,763	11,159	85,166
1,790	2,770	12,098	9,984	8,730	17,111	6,305	12,319	9,825	71,029
1,984	3,070	11,516	10,389	9,922	16,095	6,106	10,955	8,958	60,247
2,100	3,250	11,758	8,269	10,082	15,944	6,357	9,486	8,857	55,231
2,294	3,550	11,477	8,163	9,755	17,043	6,084	9,335	9,615	49,516
2,488	3,850	11,799	7,245	7,554	16,739	3,803	8,533	10,501	44,572

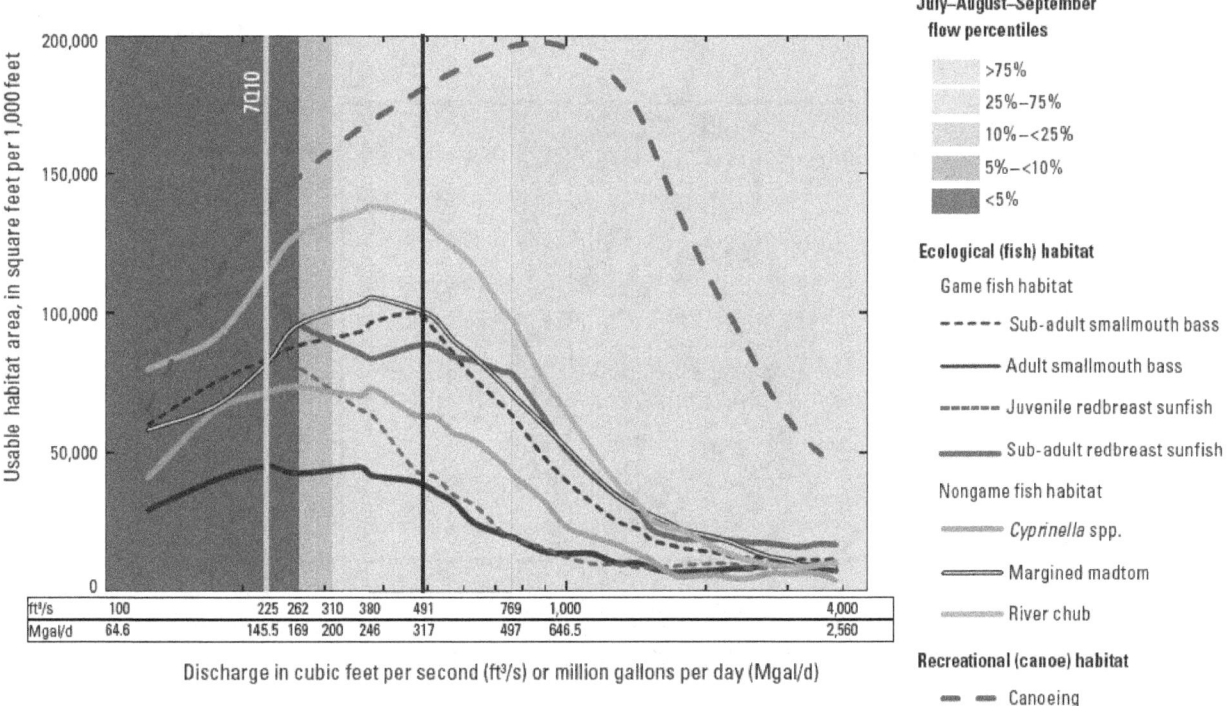

Figure 15. Weighted usable-habitat area of ecological and recreational habitat at the Kauffman Mill study reach on the South Fork of the Shenandoah River, Virginia. Flow percentiles are based on data from the Luray streamflow gaging station (01629500) from 1979 to 2008 for streamflows during the months of July, August, and September. These statistics represent the expected range of flows, based on the historic streamflow record.

the percentage of each type of habitat present in the river, WUA, was calculated for a range of streamflows from 130 to 5,160 ft³/s (table 14). The WUA for Thunderbird Farms and the Front Royal sections of river is shown in table 19 and figure 17.

To illustrate the amount of WUA commonly expected for each fish during the low-flow period, the JAS normal range of flows (420 to 830 ft³/s), the 10th percentile flow (330 ft³/s) for JAS flows, the 5th percentile flow (290 ft³/s) for JAS flows, and the annual 7Q10 statistic (247.4 ft³/s) were plotted over each set of WUA curves (fig. 17). The normal range of flows for JAS includes the maximum WUA for all fish except juvenile and sub-adult redbreast sunfish. The maximum WUA for sub-adult redbreast sunfish occurs at slightly less than the 25th percentile flow; the juvenile redbreast sunfish WUA continues to increase with decreasing discharge to the lowest flow simulated. For pool and run-dwelling fish like smallmouth bass and redbreast sunfish, habitat availability does not vary much from the normal range of flows for the low-flow period, down to the 5th percentile

flow (290 ft³/s). Below the 5th percentile, habitat sharply decreases. For riffle-dwelling fish, the normal range of flows maintains habitat availability, but below the 25th percentile flow (420 ft³/s), decreases and then remains steady (fig. 17). Habitat declines as flows decline for all species, except juvenile redbreast sunfish, as flows decrease below the annual 7Q10.

Canoeing through the Front Royal Section

Canoeing through the Front Royal section takes the paddler through the widest channels on the South Fork and extensive sections of bedrock riffle like that present in transect 4 of the Thunderbird Farms study reach, or throughout Andy Guest State Park (Krstolic and Hayes, 2010). These bedrock riffles typically run perpendicular to the flow and are usually areas of shallow-water depth. To represent adequate canoeing suitability throughout this section, transect 4 was examined in detail. RHABSIM modeling results show that the minimum flow needed to maintain an average depth greater than or equal to 1 ft is 557 ft³/s (50th percentile JAS flow),

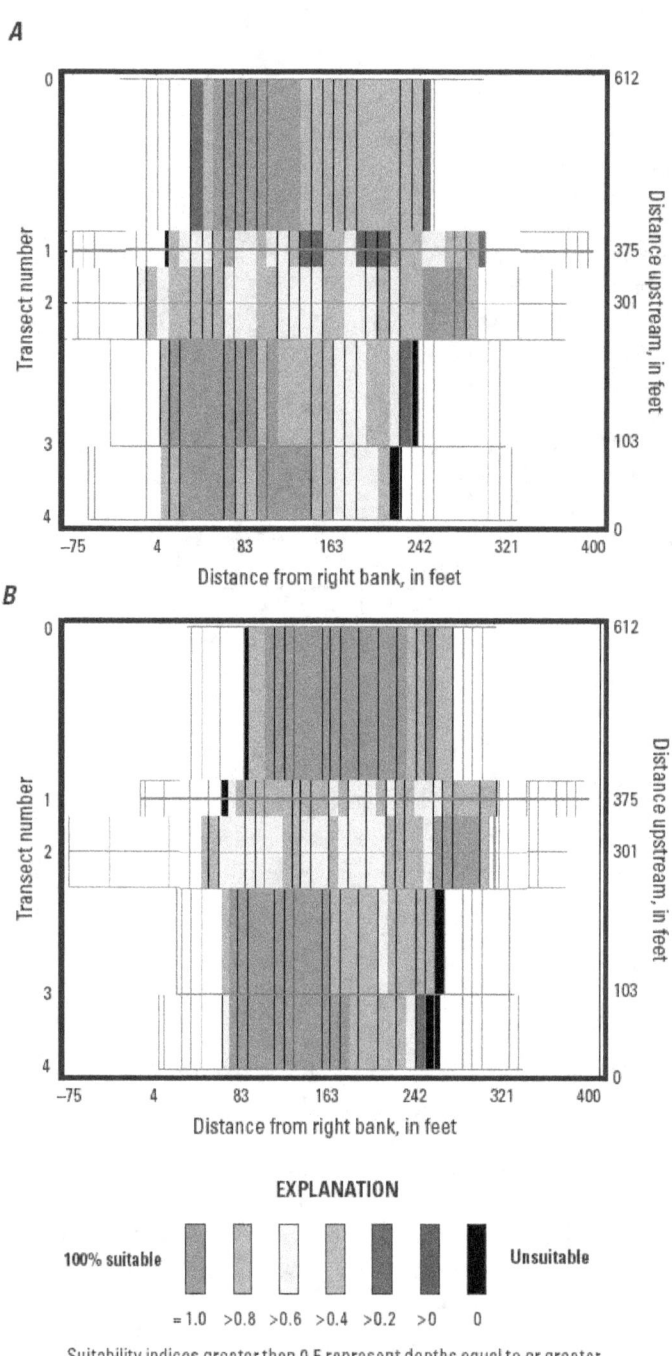

Figure 16.   Model grid of canoeing depth suitability for the Kauffman Mill study reach on the South Fork of the Shenandoah River, Virginia. *A*, 520 cubic feet per second; and *B*, 890 cubic feet per second.

Table 19.   Weighted usable-habitat area, in square feet per 1,000 feet of stream, for the Thunderbird Farms study reach on the South Fork Shenandoah River, Virginia.

[Mgal/d, million gallons per day; ft³/s, cubic feet per second]

Simulated discharge, Mgal/d	Simulated discharge, ft³/s	Ecological habitat							Recreational habitat
		Fish species							Canoeing
		Sub-adult smallmouth bass	Adult small-mouth bass	Juvenile redbreast sunfish	Sub-adult redbreast sunfish	*Cyprinella* spp.	Margined madtom	River chub	
116	179	67,074	78,247	63,581	137,844	27,384	27,685	67,815	19,202
147	228	82,051	103,090	59,826	141,063	26,112	27,685	67,986	45,060
187	290	92,037	111,543	54,082	147,624	27,062	30,810	65,698	86,310
211	327	98,800	117,935	49,318	151,019	32,640	37,827	66,442	111,613
226	349	99,237	119,360	47,753	152,973	32,661	39,944	67,192	127,612
261	404	100,757	122,957	44,642	150,962	32,292	40,421	74,491	161,079
291	450	101,158	134,361	40,101	149,028	30,668	44,275	88,490	184,831
360	557	99,539	136,537	29,804	124,686	40,276	55,827	84,775	229,761
387	599	97,207	135,187	30,700	121,897	39,168	54,529	85,485	241,543
451	698	93,053	124,338	25,531	110,154	37,524	51,199	83,390	263,244
537	831	87,990	111,994	15,061	92,280	29,857	47,717	76,312	282,499
580	897	86,327	100,986	13,342	90,323	26,522	43,117	72,172	288,851
613	948	83,194	93,889	12,503	88,796	25,340	41,003	66,933	292,700
726	1,123	64,779	71,440	8,511	82,795	19,271	35,302	52,389	298,234
784	1,213	62,225	68,782	6,828	81,543	18,704	32,114	49,498	304,162
848	1,312	57,198	63,374	6,134	77,455	17,051	27,285	44,262	306,880
913	1,412	52,724	57,478	5,325	73,306	14,381	19,319	37,669	308,701
963	1,490	50,044	52,516	5,286	71,042	13,550	15,797	33,229	309,529
1,137	1,760	36,712	26,498	3,940	59,067	7,141	11,931	19,750	311,273
1,233	1,908	31,617	18,105	3,589	52,789	6,293	11,465	15,046	311,780
1,334	2,064	25,643	11,101	2,162	37,367	4,754	10,722	14,210	314,180
1,525	2,360	19,096	7,389	2,193	31,425	2,634	8,927	9,435	308,636
1,579	2,444	18,458	7,389	2,549	30,427	2,634	8,629	8,407	307,575
1,772	2,742	14,299	6,649	2,749	21,088	2,055	5,831	4,490	302,946
2,042	3,160	6,294	3,790	1,569	7,881	1,284	4,549	2,441	292,816
2,413	3,734	3,811	1,810	1,221	6,595	771	1,928	2,055	268,418
2,734	4,230	2,037	1,818	1,290	3,335	386	1,547	781	247,716
3,005	4,650	1,826	1,409	1,224	3,864	0	971	964	226,476
3,335	5,160	1,411	2,066	839	3,499	0	386	193	199,321

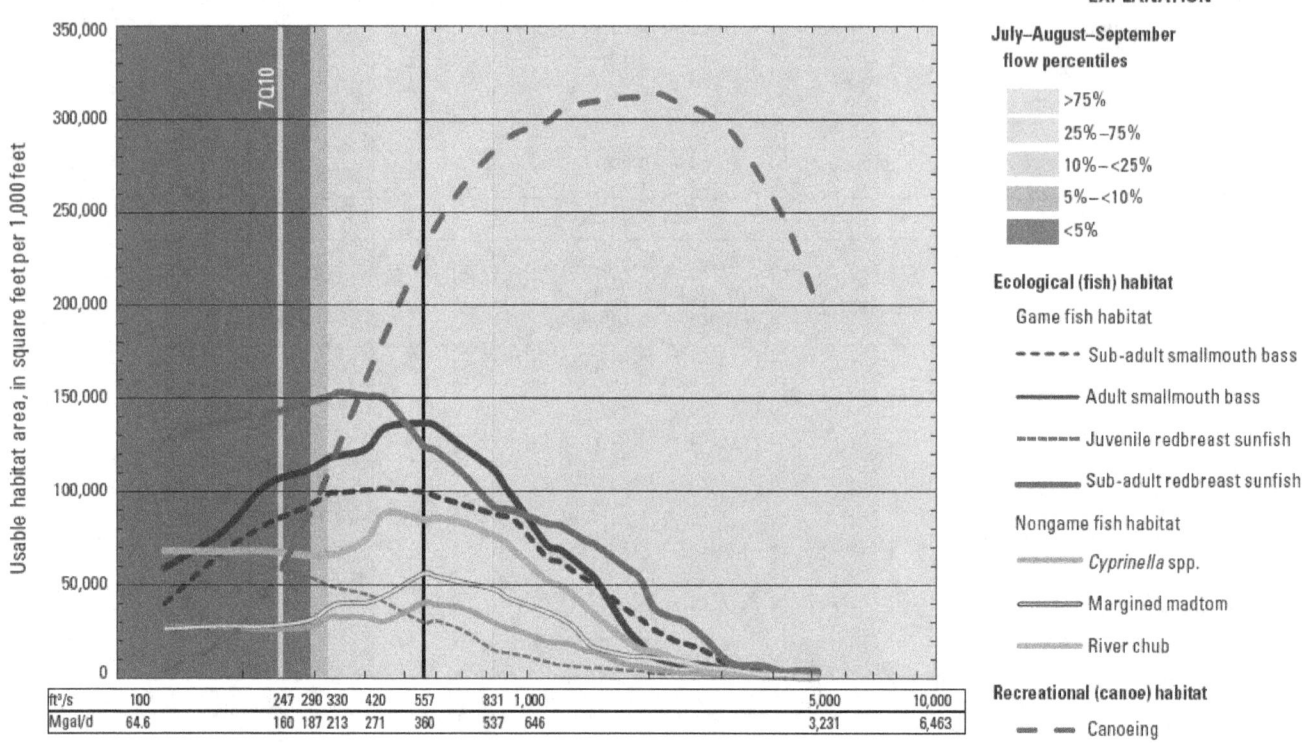

EXPLANATION

July–August–September
flow percentiles

>75%

25%–75%

10%–<25%

5%–<10%

<5%

Ecological (fish) habitat

Game fish habitat

- - - - Sub-adult smallmouth bass

——— Adult smallmouth bass

– – – – Juvenile redbreast sunfish

——— Sub-adult redbreast sunfish

Nongame fish habitat

——— *Cyprinella* spp.

——— Margined madtom

——— River chub

Recreational (canoe) habitat

— — Canoeing

Discharge in cubic feet per second (ft³/s) or million gallons per day (Mgal/d)

Figure 17. Weighted usable-habitat area of ecological and recreational habitat at Thunderbird Farms in the lower reach on the South Fork Shenandoah River, Virginia. Flow percentiles are based on data from the Front Royal streamflow-gaging station (01631000) from 1931 to 2008 for streamflows during the months of July, August, and September. These statistics represent the expected range of flows, based on the historic streamflow record.

with an average depth of 1.1 ft, a maximum depth of 1.9 ft, and an average velocity of 1.3 ft/s (fig. 18*A*). A discharge of 698 ft³/s provides an average depth of 1.3 ft, a maximum depth of 1.98 ft, and an average velocity of 1.5 ft/s, whereas a discharge of 831 ft³/s (75th percentile JAS flow) provides an average depth of 1.4 ft, a maximum depth of 2.1 ft, and an average velocity of 1.6 ft/s (fig. 18*B*). Considering the fact that this kind of habitat is typically a series of bedrock ledges of varying depth, a paddler may have more success with flows that have average depths equal to or greater than 1.4 ft. Outfitter suggestions presented in the Luray section also apply to the Front Royal section (Downriver Canoe Co., 2011). Modeling results show that the maximum suitable canoeing habitat occurs at 2,064 ft³/s (fig. 17, table 19), and as flows increase velocity suitability decreases. Average and maximum velocities associated with a discharge of 3,160 ft³/s at transect 4 are 3.1 and 4.8 ft/s respectively. When depth and velocity are considered, a suitable range for canoeing may be from 831 up to 3,160 ft³/s.

Don Hayes measures flow in a riffle at
Kauffman Mill during August 2009

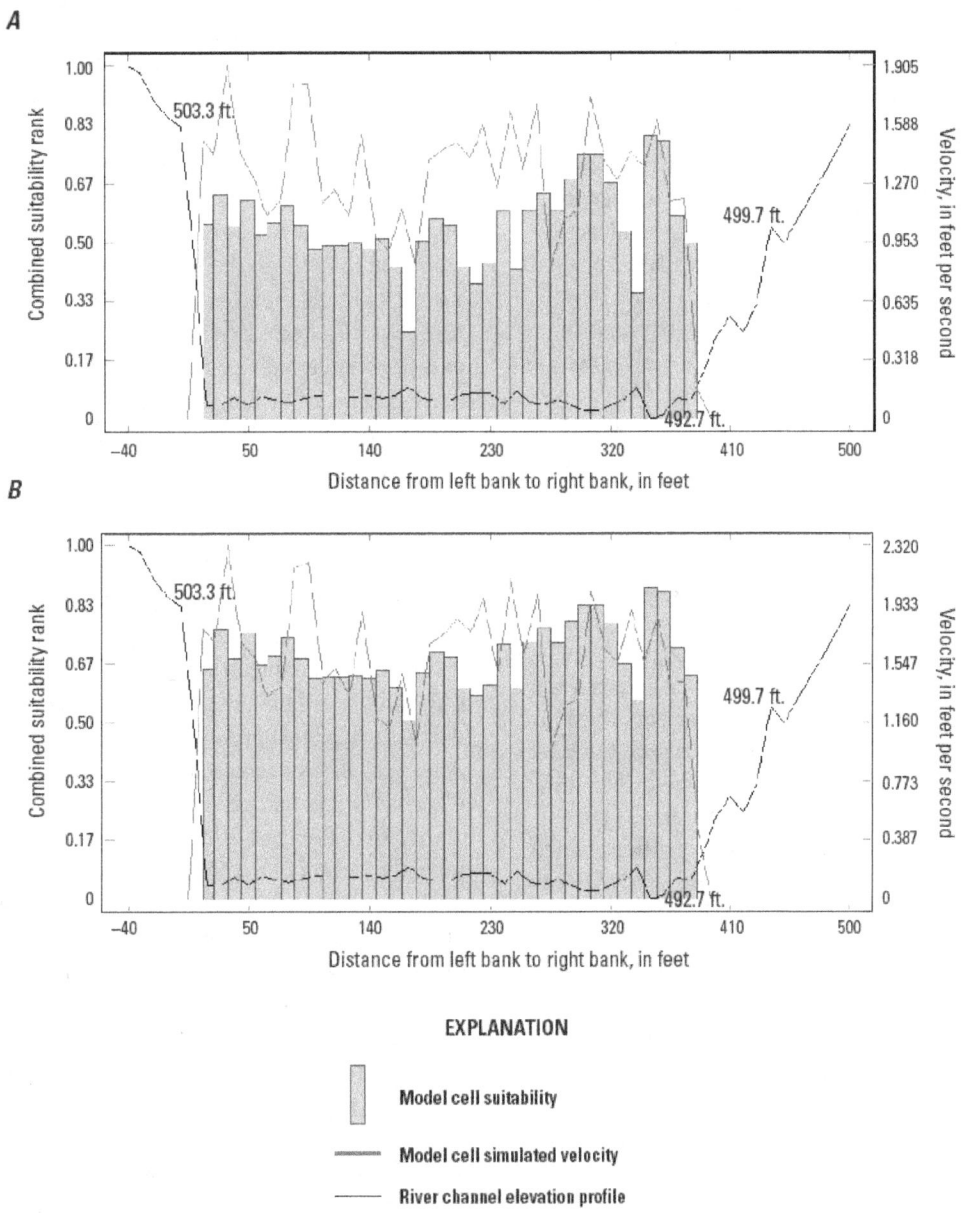

Figure 18. Canoeing suitability for the bedrock riffle at transect 4 at the Thunderbird Farms study reach on the South Fork Shenandoah River, Virginia. Combined depth and velocity suitability ranks (bars) and simulated velocity (green line) at a discharge of A, 557 cubic feet per second; and B, 831 cubic feet per second.

Habitat Time-Series Scenario Analysis for Low-Flow Periods

Time-series plots of the habitat availability can be calculated from the discharge-habitat relations and applied to historic daily flows for streamflow-gaging stations on the South Fork to provide a picture of habitat availability over all flows measured. Drought years were examined as examples of times when habitat was potentially limited so that species and habitats affected by drought could be identified. This assessment sought to describe the flow conditions that were potentially stressful for each species or lifestage and to describe normal or ideal conditions related to habitat availability. The results and descriptions are interpretations of the weighted usable-habitat area curves, the time-series plots, and the historic flow record. The scenarios presented in this report are for informational purposes only, and any final selection of flow thresholds and desired habitat availability during drought or low-flow periods would belong to the purview of managers, planners, and policymakers in the Shenandoah Valley.

Historic droughts represent rare conditions that require planning and preparation to ensure enough water availability for citizens and to maintain healthy rivers. Five historic summer drought low-flow periods (1932, 1966, 1977, 1999, and 2002) were examined for each study site when data were available. The most extreme drought on record occurred in 2002, so that year was used for time-series examples for each river section. Other time periods were presented when they helped define thresholds or the effects of water withdrawal scenarios. For withdrawal scenarios, river conditions had to reach extreme lows (less than 10th or 5th percentile JAS flow) before withdrawal increases or water-conservation scenarios showed noticeable effect on habitat availability.

During historic droughts, adequate flows for canoeing rarely occurred. For instance, along the middle section of the South Fork, flows less than the 25th percentile flow for JAS do not provide adequate depth for passage through riffle habitats. For the time-series scenarios presented in this report, flow conditions were between the 25th and 5th percentile JAS flows, but generally less than the 10th percentile flow for JAS. Although recreation is certainly a consideration for water-resources management, when flows are far below the 25th percentile and decreasing, canoe paddling is unlikely to be successful, even with reduced water withdrawals.

Upper Section Time-Series Scenarios

The upper section of the South Fork flows from the confluence of the North, Middle, and South Rivers to the Shenandoah Dam Reservoir. The annual median flow for this section of river is 604 ft³/s (390.4 Mgal/d, table 2). The normal range of flows for JAS is 265 to 544 ft³/s (171.3 to 351.6 Mgal/d, table 2). Habitat time-series plots for game and nongame fish during 2002 and 1977 are presented in figures 19 and 20.

Streamflows were below normal from June 1, 2002, to October 1, 2002; the discharge ranged from 448 to 84 ft³/s with all but 12 days less than 265 ft³/s (the 25th percentile flow for JAS). This time period represents an extreme drought scenario for the Lynnwood streamflow-gaging station. Maximum WUA values occur just below the 25th percentile JAS flow for nongame fish, and within the normal range of flows for all game fish except juvenile redbreast sunfish (fig. 11, table 15). During 2002, habitat availability for all species, except juvenile redbreast sunfish, decreased between 40 to 70 percent for a given species when flows decreased from 200 to 84 ft³/s. Beginning June 15, 2002, when streamflow at the Lynnwood gage was 205 ft³/s (about 10th percentile flow; fig. 19), decreases in habitat occurred for all species except juvenile redbreast sunfish. Figure 19 shows expected normal range of habitat availability, or JAS weighted usable-habitat area percentiles, as well as the time-series results for 2002. The JAS weighted usable-habitat area percentiles represent a historic summary (such as exceedance values for streamflows) of habitat throughout JAS. The 50th percentile or median habitat condition is shown as well as the normal habitat range (25th to 75th percentile of habitat). These habitat percentiles illustrate that habitat availability during 2002 generally was less than the median for JAS and during the driest times less than the 25th habitat percentile. The habitat decrease was most pronounced in early July and mid-August as flows decreased below 100 ft³/s. In the upper reach *Cyprinella* spp. and sub-adult redbreast sunfish habitat availability were the least affected by low-flow conditions. This is the only section of the South Fork that showed even marginal declines in sub-adult redbreast sunfish habitat. Flows less than 100 ft³/s are much less than the 5th percentile of flow for JAS (178 ft³/s, table 2) and are typically rare; however, time-series data from 2002 show that extreme low-flow conditions corresponded to below-normal habitat availability for both game and nongame fish for extended periods of time in the upper section of the river.

Streamflows during 1977 remained near the 10th percentile JAS flow for 62 days, and below the 5th percentile for 26 days, which represent a less intense drought than 2002. Habitat time-series comparisons between 2002 and 1977 (figs. 19, 20), showed that the 10th percentile flow (203 ft³/s) was an indicator of some habitat limitation, but when flows remained at the 10th percentile, as they did in 1977, habitat area did not decrease greatly. JAS weighted usable-habitat area percentiles overlaid on figure 20 confirm that habitat conditions were close to the 50th percentile for most days in 1977. Habitat time-series simulations only resulted in a decrease for adult smallmouth bass during 1977 (fig. 20).

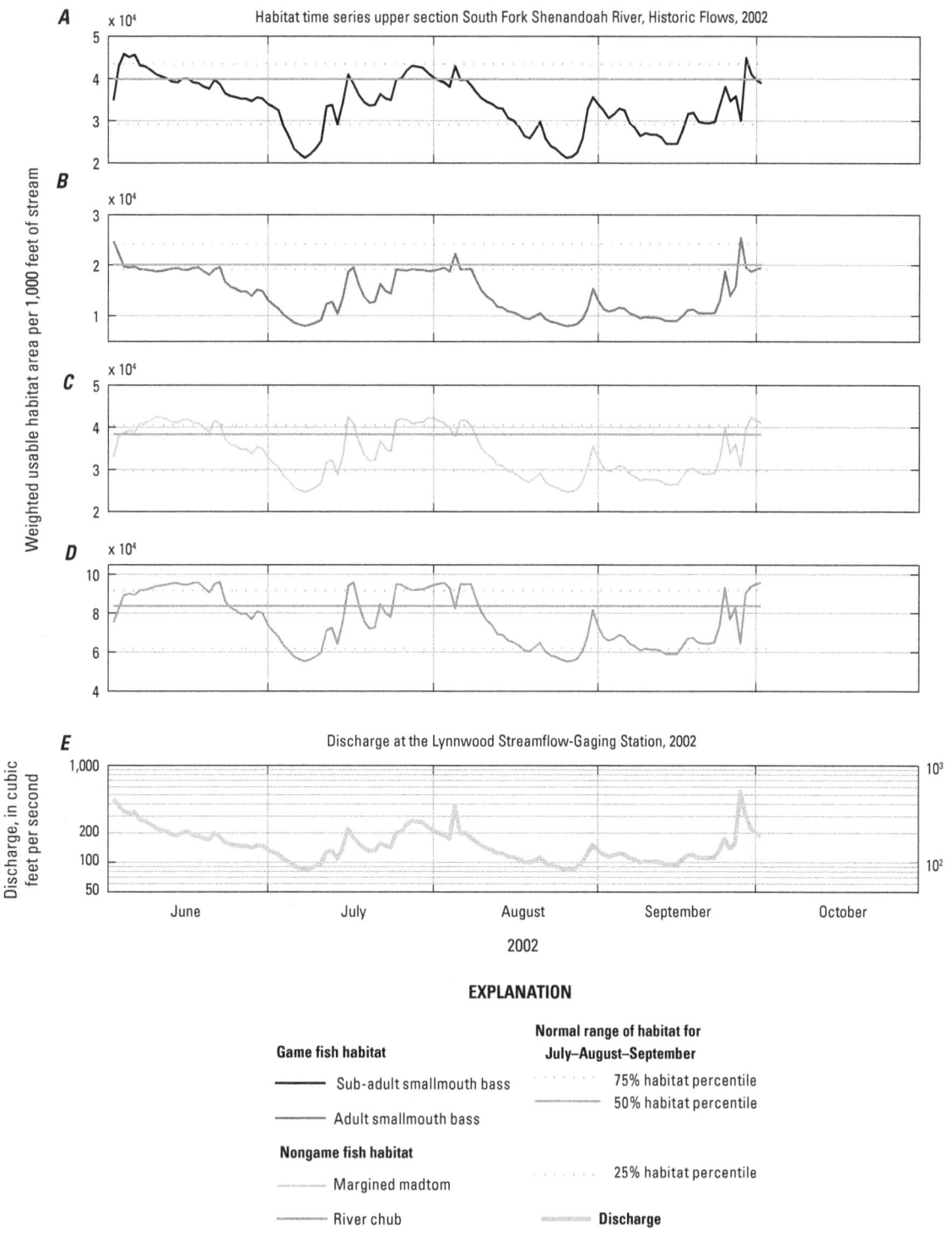

Figure 19. Habitat time series for the upper section of the South Fork Shenandoah River near Lynnwood, Virginia, during 2002. *A* and *B*, game fish weighted usable-habitat area; *C* and *D*, nongame fish weighted usable-habitat area; and *E*, daily mean discharge for the river near Lynnwood (01628500).

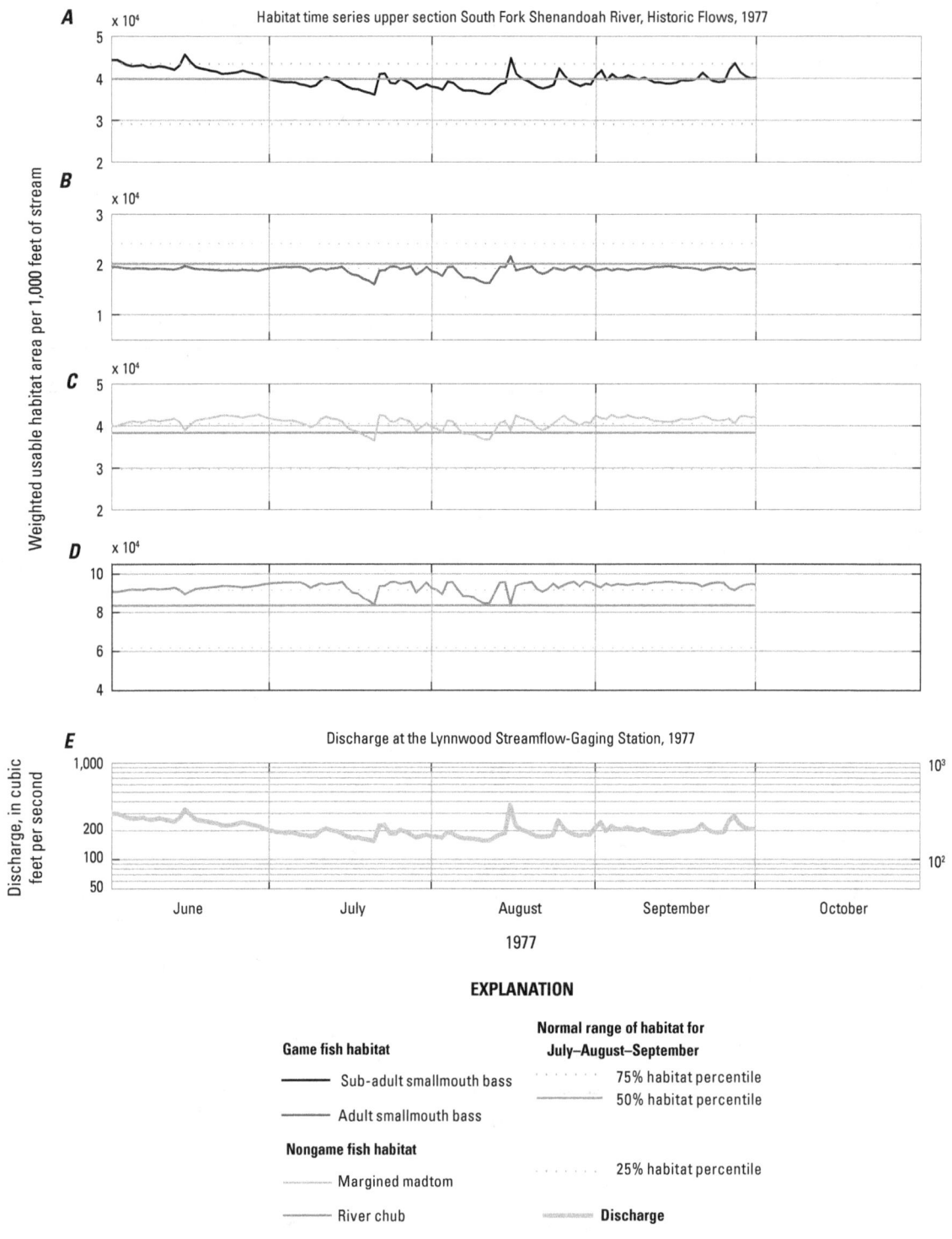

Figure 20.   Habitat time series for the upper section of the South Fork Shenandoah River near Lynnwood, Virginia, during 1977. *A* and *B*, game fish weighted usable-habitat area; *C* and *D*, nongame fish weighted usable-habitat area; and *E*, daily mean discharge for the river near Lynnwood (01628500).

Middle Section Time-Series Scenarios

The middle section of the South Fork flows from the Shenandoah Dam to the Luray Dam. The annual median flow for this section of river is 828 ft^3/s (535.2 Mgal/d, table 2). The normal range of flows for JAS is 380 to 769 ft^3/s (245.6 to 497 Mgal/d, table 2). Combined habitat time-series plots for selected species or lifestages during 2002 and 1999 are presented (figs. 21, 22).

Streamflows were below normal from June 1, 2002, to October 1, 2002; the discharge ranged from 163 to 624 ft^3/s with all but 12 days less than the 25th percentile flow for JAS (380 ft^3/s, fig. 21). During 2002, habitat availability decreased for all species except juvenile redbreast sunfish and sub-adult redbreast sunfish. Because adult smallmouth bass, margined madtom, and river chub maximum WUA all occurred in association with the 25th percentile flow (fig. 15), a decrease in streamflow below 380 ft^3/s corresponded with a decrease in habitat availability. The greatest decrease in habitat availability for smallmouth bass, sub-adult smallmouth bass, margined madtom, and river chub occurred between July 1, 2002, and July 26, 2002, when flows decreased below the 5th percentile of flow for JAS (262 ft^3/s, fig. 21). In the middle reach, the habitat discharge relation shows about a 10-percent reduction in available habitat for each species between the 25th percentile and the 5th percentile flow. The JAS weighted usable-habitat area percentiles for habitat summary statistics and time-series habitat simulations for summer drought are shown in figure 21. During the lowest flows in 2002, margined madtom and river chub habitat area were lower than the 25th habitat percentile, whereas adult and sub-adult smallmouth bass habitat area were lower than the 50th percentile. In this reach, juvenile redbreast sunfish and sub-adult redbreast sunfish habitat were unaffected by low-flow conditions.

During 1999, streamflows were less than the 5th percentile JAS flow (262 ft^3/s) for 47 days, but never dropped below 200 ft^3/s between May 16, 1999, and September 5, 1999 (fig. 22). During these flow conditions, the habitat area decrease was not as drastic as in 2002. Habitat availability decreased slightly below the 50th habitat percentile for sub-adult smallmouth bass, margined madtom, and river chub in August, but did not decrease below the 25th habitat percentile (fig. 22). No decrease in habitat area occurred for *Cyprinella* spp., smallmouth bass, juvenile redbreast sunfish, or sub-adult redbreast sunfish. In the middle section, as demonstrated by the 1999 drought, when flows remain above the 5th percentile JAS flow, habitat is not expected to decrease greatly.

Lower Section Time-Series Scenarios

The lower section of the South Fork is the largest section of river, ending at the confluence of the North Fork and South Fork near Front Royal. The annual median flow for this section of river is 948 ft^3/s (612.7 Mgal/d, table 2). The normal range of flows for JAS is 420 to 831 ft^3/s (271.5 to 537.1 Mgal/d, table 2). Combined habitat time-series plots for selected species or lifestages during 2002 and 1966 are presented (figs. 23, 24).

Streamflows were below normal from June 1, 2002, to October 1, 2002; the discharge ranged from 164 to 709 ft^3/s with all but 11 days less than the 25th percentile flow (420 ft^3/s, fig. 23). The maximum WUA for smallmouth bass, sub-adult smallmouth bass, margined madtom, *Cyprinella* spp., and river chub is associated with flows greater than the 25th percentile JAS flow between 450 and 557 ft^3/s (table 19). During 2002, habitat availability decreased slightly for all species except juvenile redbreast sunfish and sub-adult redbreast sunfish. The adult smallmouth bass, sub-adult smallmouth bass, and margined madtom habitat area were lower than 25th habitat percentile, and less than the normal range (fig. 23). This habitat decrease occurred when flows were below 300 ft^3/s, which occurred three times for at least 6 days during this period. All other species of fish had habitat availability within the normal range for JAS. River chub habitat availability during 2002 had a slightly different pattern than the other species. As flows decreased below 450 ft^3/s, habitat availability remained steady slightly higher than the 25th habitat percentile. No major decreases occurred for river chub habitat when flows decreased below 300 or 200 ft^3/s; however, the habitat was less than would be available within the normal range of flows (fig. 23, table 19).

Similar patterns are shown in time-series plots for 1966 as flows decreased below 200 ft^3/s and eventually below 130 ft^3/s (the lowest simulated flow for this section of river; fig. 24). The time-series plots of habitat availability for game and nongame fish differed with very low flows during 1966. The smallmouth bass and sub-adult smallmouth bass habitat area continued to decrease as flows decreased (fig. 24); however, the river chub, and margined madtom habitat area remained constant as flows decreased less than 300 ft^3/s (figs. 17, 24). In combination, the WUA and time-series plots illustrate that as flows decrease below the 25th percentile JAS flow to the 5th percentile flow in the lower section of the South Fork, habitat availability for game fish (except juvenile redbreast sunfish) will continue to decrease, but habitat availability for nongame fish remains below normal, but stable.

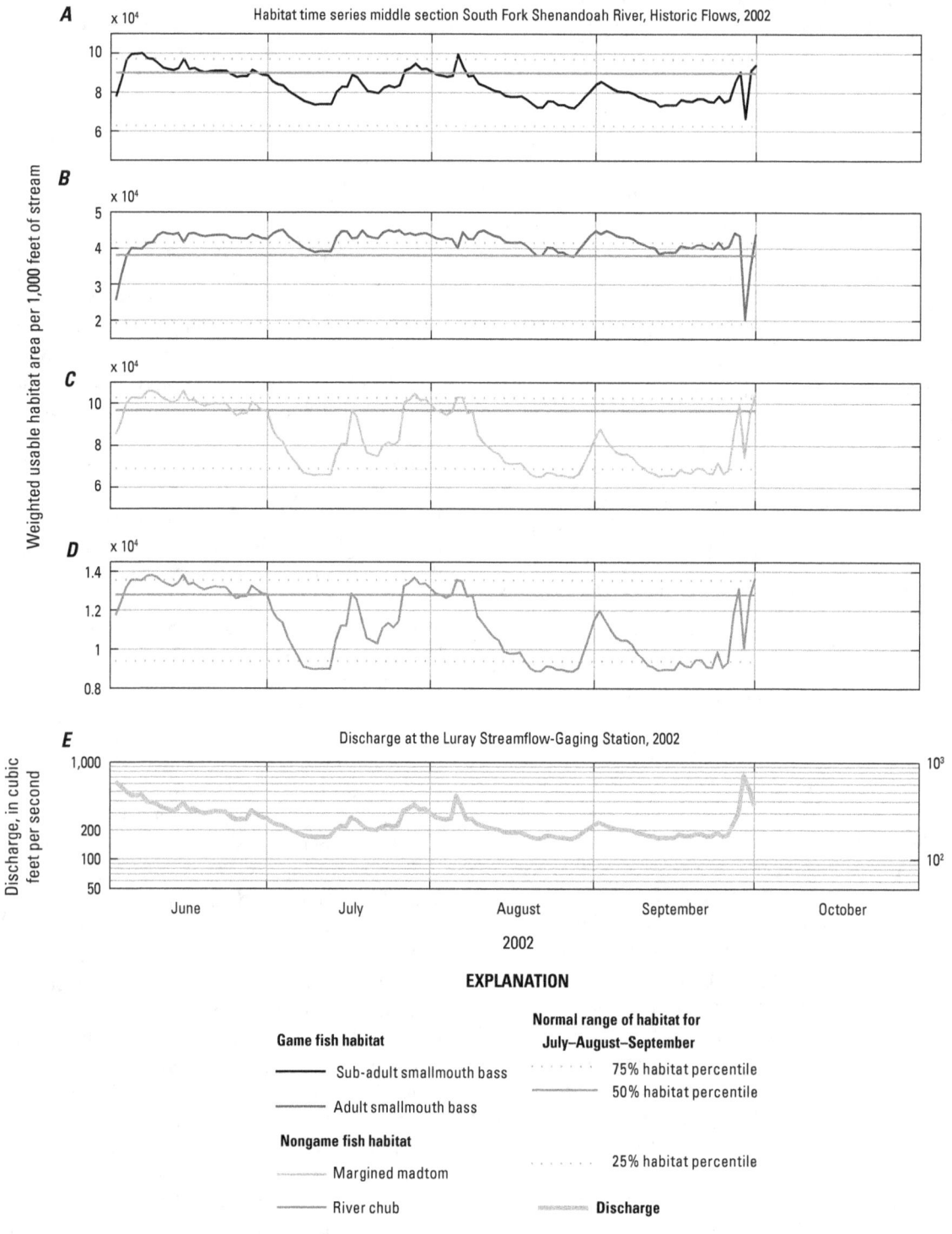

Figure 21. Habitat time series for the middle section of the South Fork Shenandoah River near Luray, Virginia, during 2002. *A* and *B*, game fish weighted usable-habitat area; *C* and *D*, nongame fish weighted usable-habitat area; and *E*, daily mean discharge for the river near Luray (01629500).

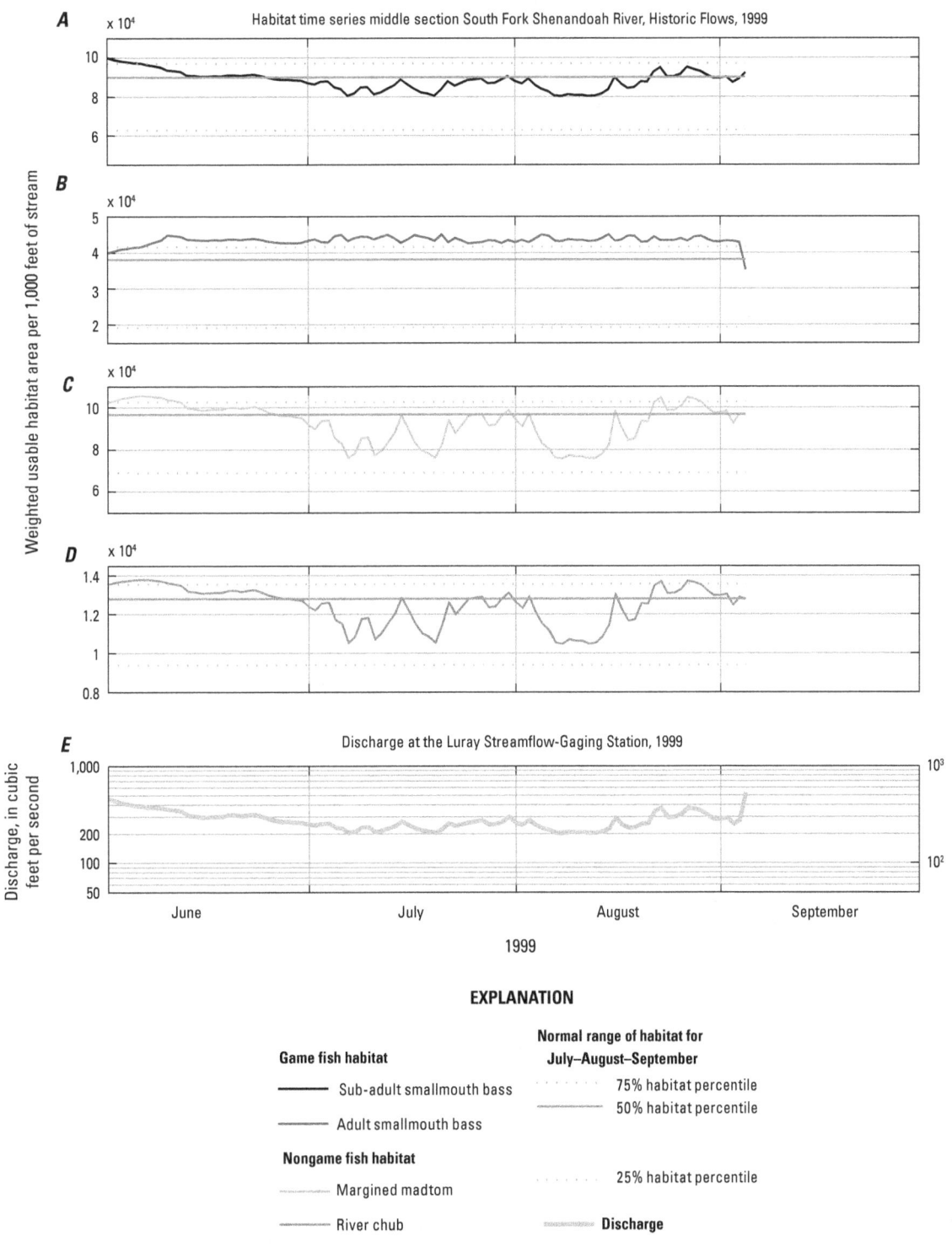

Figure 22. Habitat time series for the middle section of the South Fork Shenandoah River near Luray, Virginia, during 1999. *A* and *B*, game fish weighted usable-habitat area; *C* and *D*, nongame fish weighted usable-habitat area; and *E*, daily mean discharge for the river near Luray (01629500).

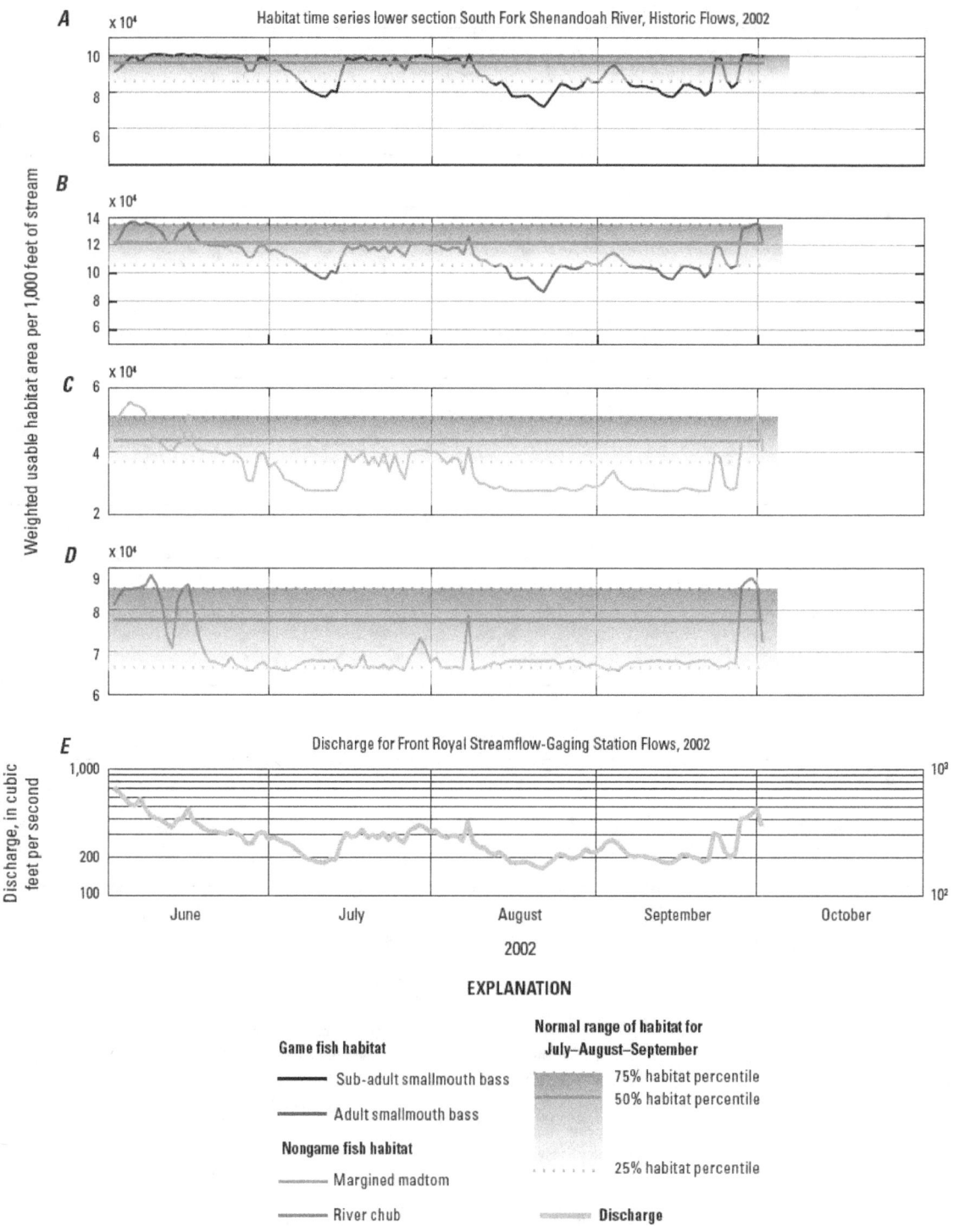

Figure 23. Habitat time series for the lower section of the South Fork Shenandoah River near Front Royal, Virginia, during 2002. *A* and *B*, game fish weighted usable-habitat area; *C* and *D*, nongame fish weighted usable-habitat area; and *E*, daily mean discharge for the river at Front Royal (01631000).

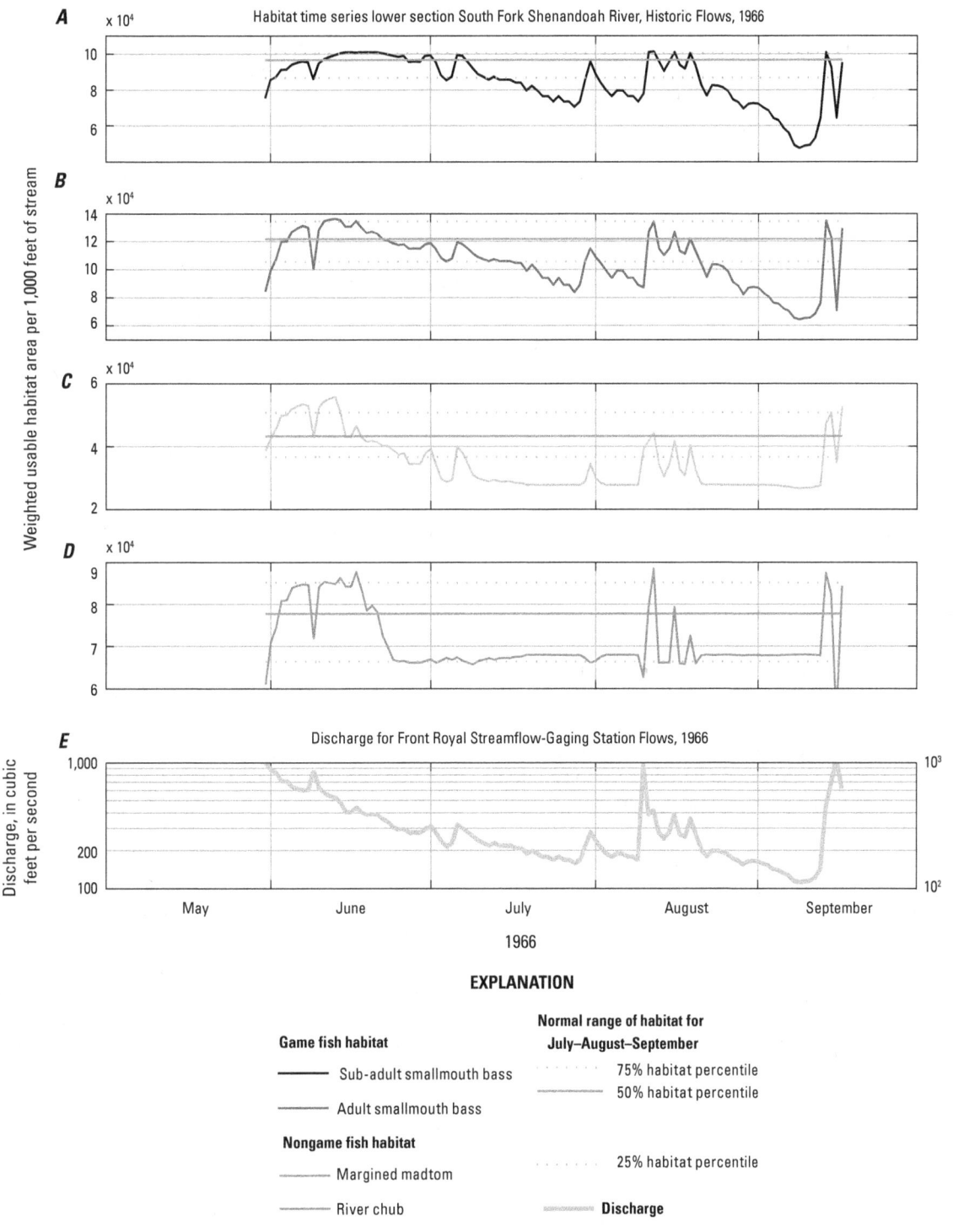

Figure 24. Habitat time series for the lower section of the South Fork Shenandoah River near Front Royal, Virginia, during 1966. *A* and *B*, game fish weighted usable-habitat area; *C* and *D*, nongame fish weighted usable-habitat area; and *E*, daily mean discharge for the river at Front Royal (01631000).

Water-Withdrawal Reduction Scenario Results

Reductions in water withdrawals were simulated for 2002 to model potential water-conservation strategies that could be implemented during a drought for each section of the South Fork (figs. 25–27). Withdrawal reductions that were simulated were percentages of the published 2005 withdrawal amounts for each section shown in table 4. Simulation results for 2002 were fairly similar regardless of river section, so they were summarized together. Habitat availability for game fish was below normal in the 2002 time series before any withdrawal scenarios were considered. With 10- or 20-percent reduced water withdrawals, minor increases in habitat availability were observed (figs. 25–27). For game fish, 50-percent water-withdrawal reductions resulted in habitat availability within the normal range for habitat in the upper and middle river sections (figs. 25–26). For nongame fish such as river chub, 20-percent withdrawal reductions resulted in habitat conditions within the normal range in the upper and middle river sections, but in the lower section near Front Royal, nongame habitat availability did not increase much with any water-withdrawal reduction scenario simulated for 2002 (fig. 27). In the same section, habitat availability for nongame fish stabilized near the 25th habitat percentile and very little change in physical habitat area was simulated regardless of withdrawal scenario.

Water withdrawal scenarios were run for 2002 to assess canoeing habitat availability during low-flow periods. As with the fish habitat assessments, 10-, 20-, and 50-percent reduction in water withdrawals for 2002 were simulated, and the resulting habitat conservation options are presented in figure 28A as an example of the general results for all sections. The 10- and 20-percent reductions in withdrawals show almost no difference in WUA for canoeing, and the 50-percent reduction only provides a minimal increase in canoeing suitability. For example, streamflows in 2002 for the upper river section (fig. 28) were less than 264 ft^3/s most of the time and did not increase greater than 300 ft^3/s for much of the time period. Because flows equal to 460 ft^3/s are necessary to ensure passage in riffles, little gain for recreation would be expected even with a 50-percent reduction of withdrawals during periods similar to the 2002 simulations.

Increased Water-Use Scenario Results

Assuming that future population growth will match the 12-percent growth of the previous 10 years, water use is expected to increase likewise in the Shenandoah Valley. To demonstrate the potential effects of increased water use from the South Fork, scenarios representing an increase in surface-water use were simulated at 5, 20, and 50 percent. As with the withdrawal reduction scenarios, one game species and one nongame species are presented in the figures to represent the effects that increased water use may have on habitat availability (figs. 29–31). For the upper section, the 50-percent simulation results appear to show a bottom threshold for habitat availability; however, this is an artifact of the model simulating flows lower than the lowest modeled streamflow of 72 ft^3/s for the upper reach at Lynnwood. For most species, habitat availability was below normal in the 2002 time-series simulations. Increases of 5-percent water withdrawals resulted in a slight reduction in habitat availability; however, 20- and 50-percent withdrawals resulted in reductions of habitat substantially less than the 25th habitat percentile, or below normal for game fish in all sections of the river and for nongame fish in the upper and middle sections (figs. 29–31). When daily streamflows were higher than the 10th percentile JAS flow, habitat availability for game fish and nongame fish was much less sensitive to 5-percent increased water-use scenarios than when daily streamflows were less than the 10th percentile flow (figs. 29–31). These scenarios show that for normal or slightly dry years, increased water use is not likely to correspond with extensive habitat loss for game fish or nongame fish; however, during drought years, 20- to 50-percent increased water use may affect game fish habitat availability for all sections and nongame fish habitat availability in the upper and middle sections of the river. For nongame fish, no major reductions of habitat area were associated with increased water-use scenarios in the lower section.

To demonstrate the potential effects of increased water use on recreation during drought, scenarios representing an increase in surface-water use were simulated at 5, 20, and 50 percent. For canoeing suitability (fig. 28B), increases in water withdrawals resulted in very small decreases in available habitat, except when streamflows were already less than the 5th percentile flow for JAS. However, the flow range simulated for 2002 generally represents unsuitable conditions for recreation.

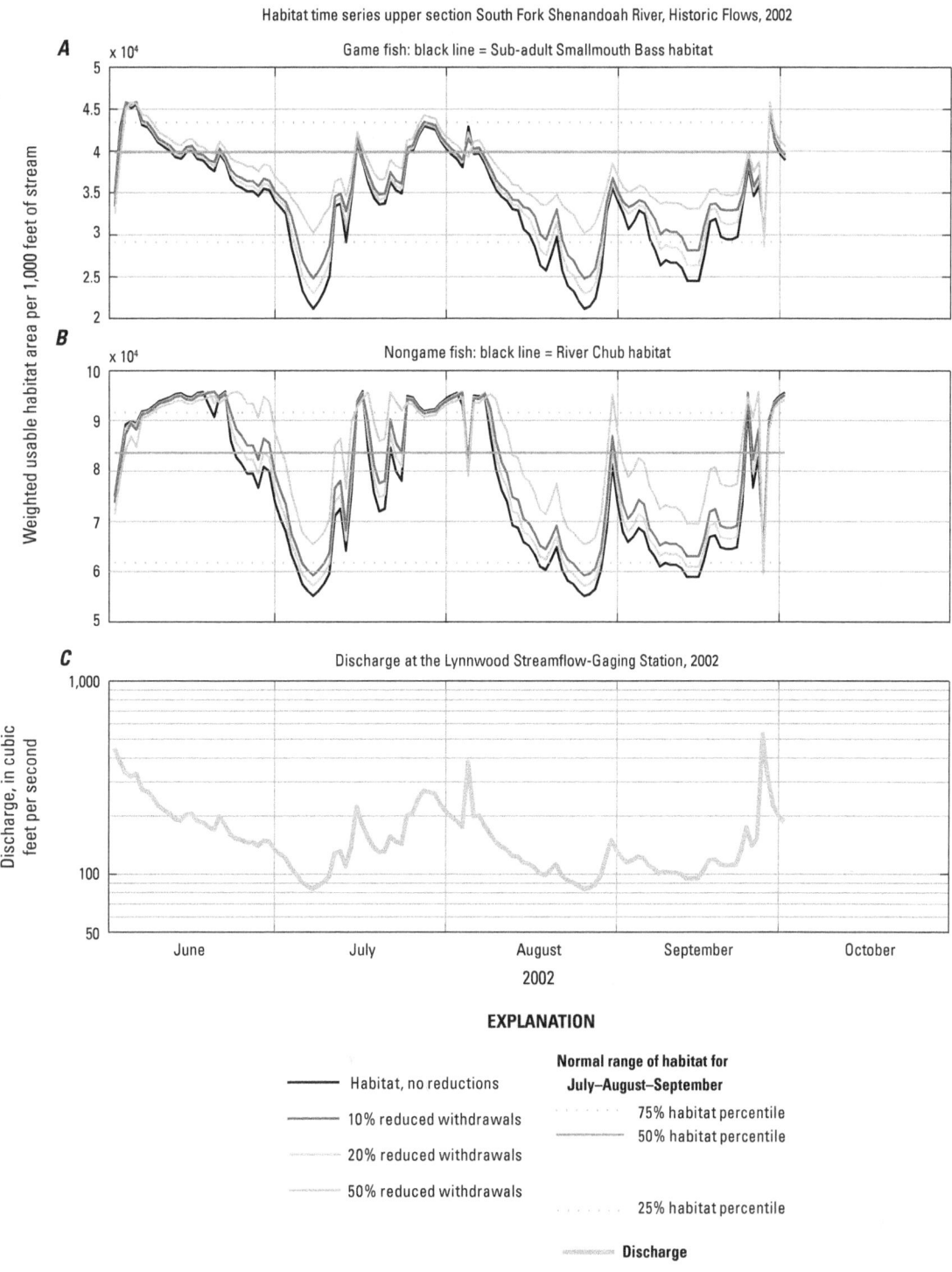

Figure 25. Habitat time-series water-withdrawal reduction scenarios for the upper section of the South Fork Shenandoah River near Lynnwood, Virginia, during 2002. *A*, sub-adult smallmouth bass weighted usable-habitat area with 10-, 20-, and 50-percent reduction in water withdrawals; *B*, river chub weighted usable-habitat area with 10-, 20-, and 50-percent reduction in water withdrawals; and *C*, daily mean discharge for the river near Lynnwood (01628500).

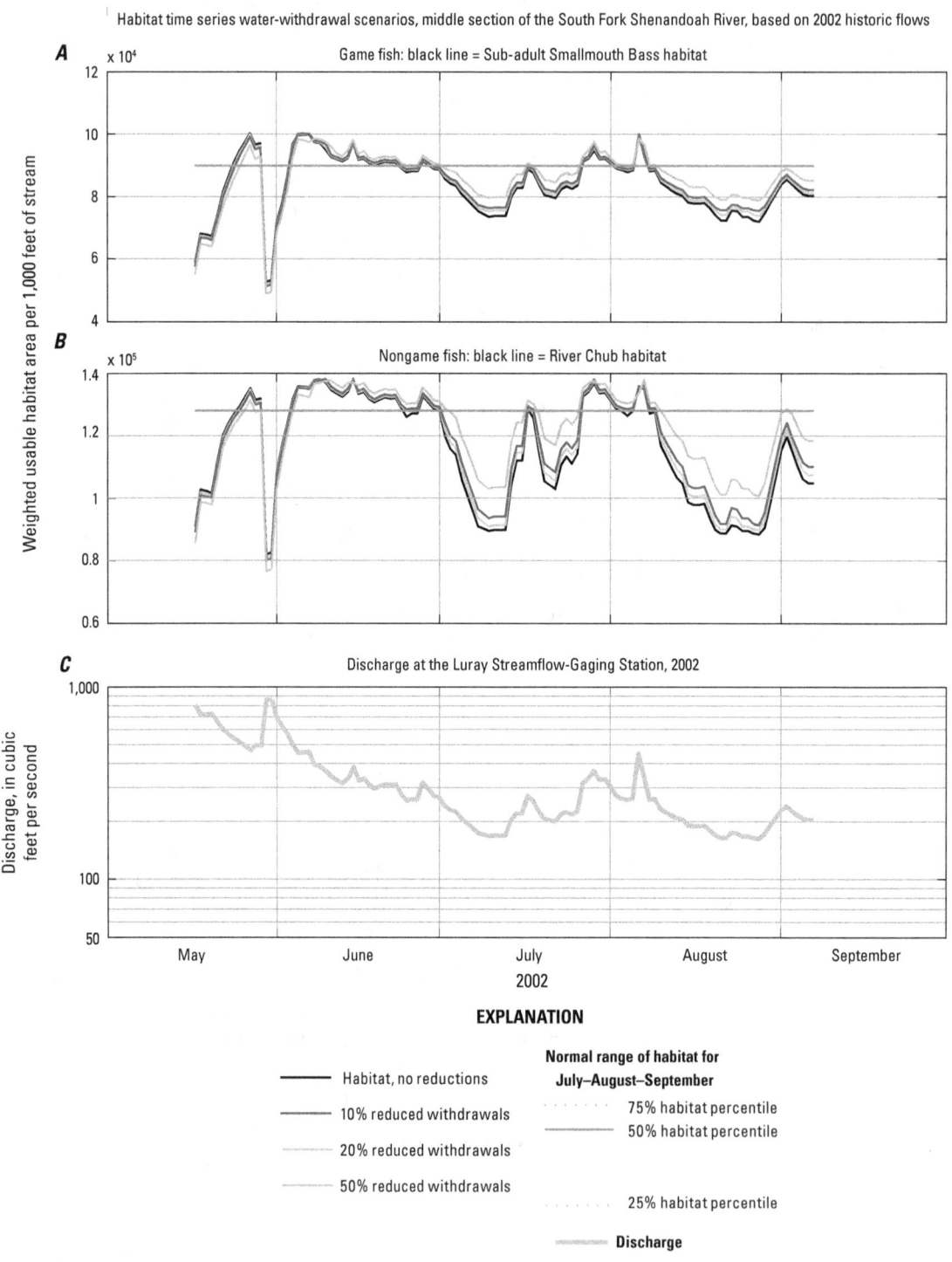

Figure 26.   Habitat time-series water-withdrawal reduction scenarios for the middle section of the South Fork Shenandoah River near Luray, Virginia, during 2002. *A,* sub-adult smallmouth bass weighted usable-habitat area with 10-, 20-, and 50-percent reduction in water withdrawals; *B,* river chub weighted usable-habitat area with 10-, 20-, and 50-percentreduction in water withdrawals; and *C,* daily mean discharge for the river near Luray (01629500).

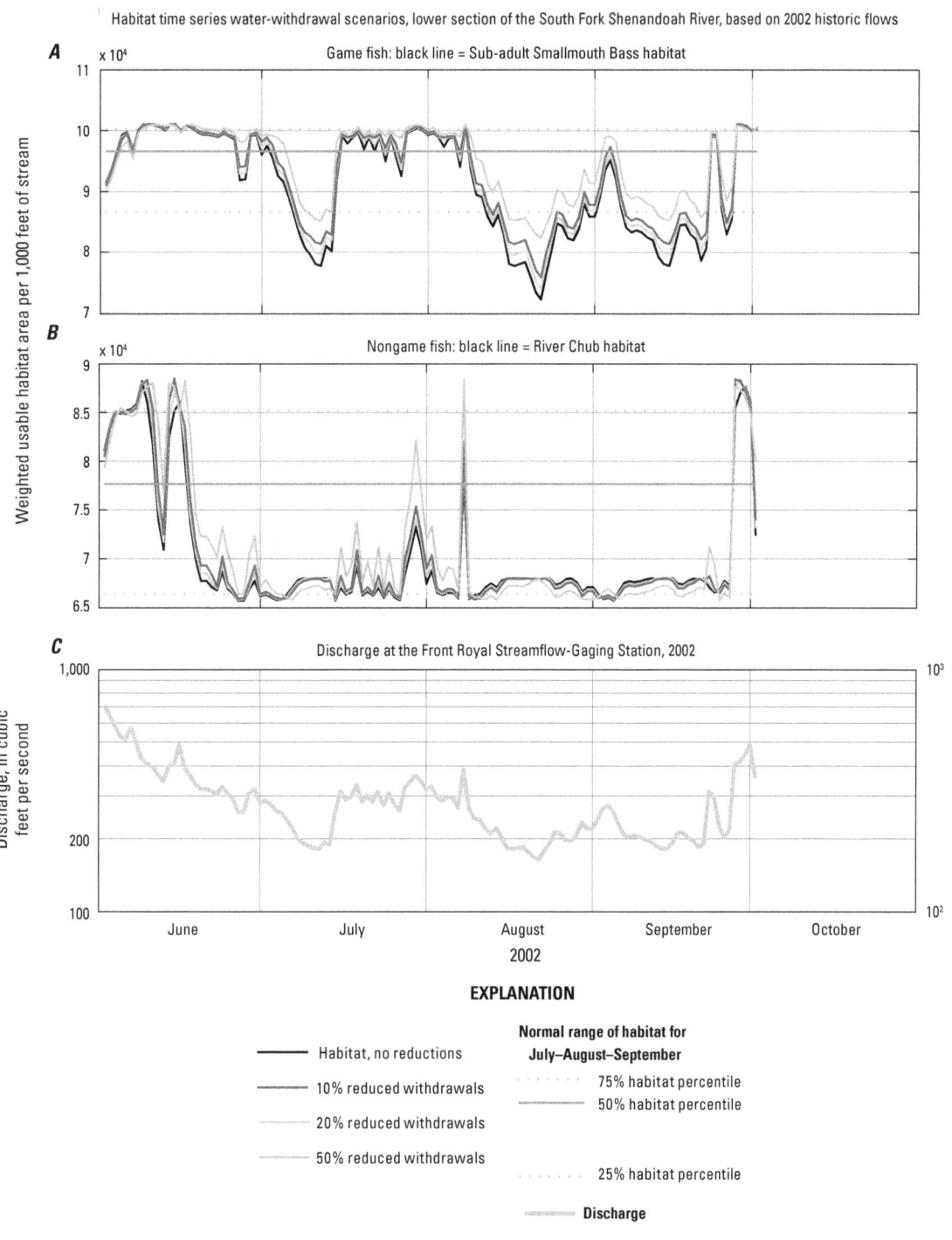

Figure 27. Habitat time-series water-withdrawal reduction scenarios for the lower section of the South Fork Shenandoah River near Front Royal, Virginia, during 2002. *A*, sub-adult smallmouth bass weighted usable-habitat area for 10-, 20-, and 50-percentreduction in water withdrawals; *B*, river chub weighted usable-habitat area with 10-, 20-, and 50-percent reduction in water withdrawals; and *C*, daily mean discharge for the river at Front Royal (01631000).

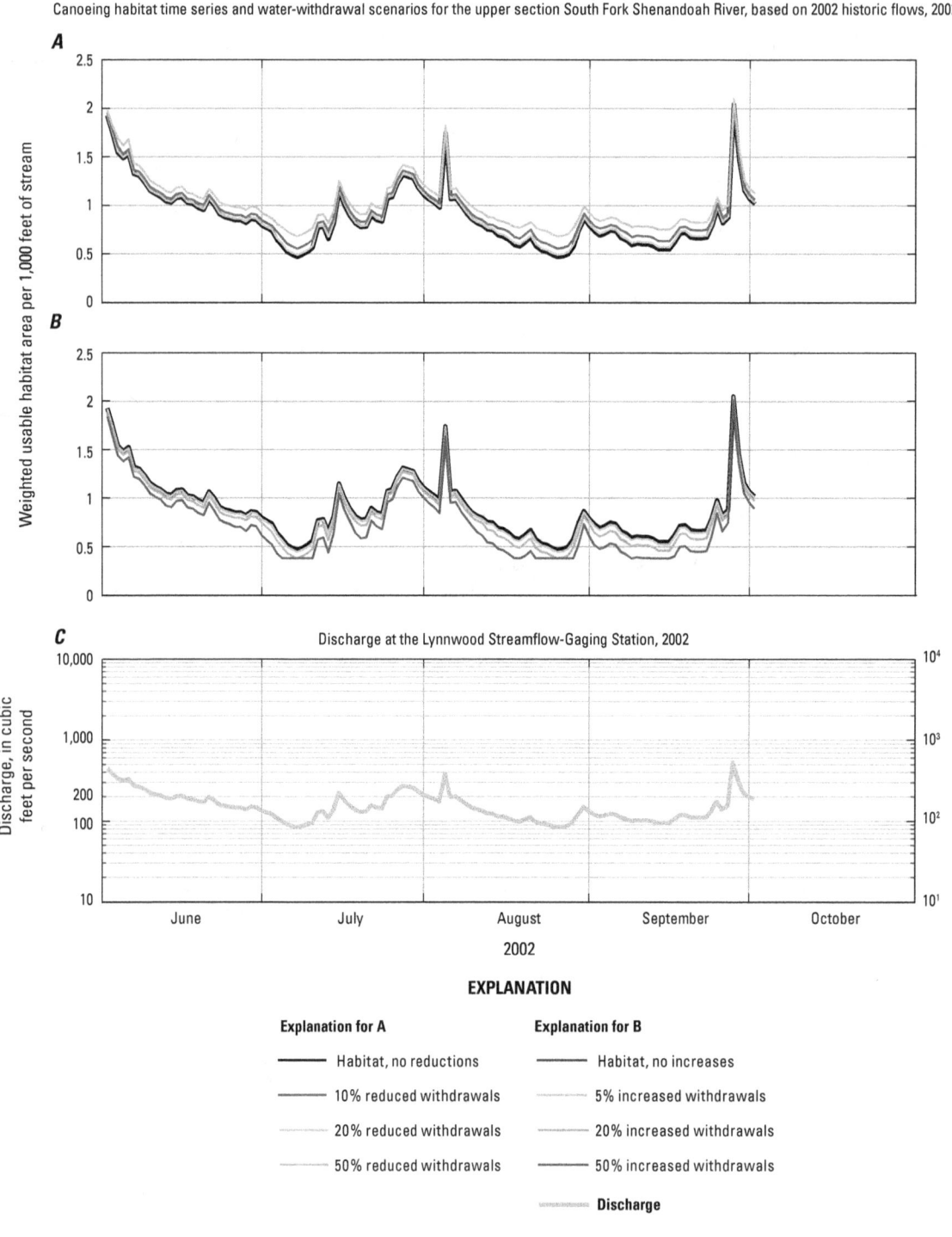

Canoeing habitat time series and water-withdrawal scenarios for the upper section South Fork Shenandoah River, based on 2002 historic flows, 2002

EXPLANATION

Explanation for A
— Habitat, no reductions
— 10% reduced withdrawals
— 20% reduced withdrawals
— 50% reduced withdrawals

Explanation for B
— Habitat, no increases
— 5% increased withdrawals
— 20% increased withdrawals
— 50% increased withdrawals
— **Discharge**

Figure 28.   Canoeing habitat time-series water-withdrawal reduction scenarios and habitat time-series increased water-withdrawal scenarios for the upper section of the South Fork Shenandoah River near Lynnwood, Virginia, during 2002. *A*, canoeing weighted usable-habitat area for 10, 20, and 50 percent decrease in water withdrawals; *B*, canoeing weighted usable-habitat area for 5-, 20-, and 50-percent increase in water use; and *C*, daily mean discharge for the river near Lynnwood (01628500).

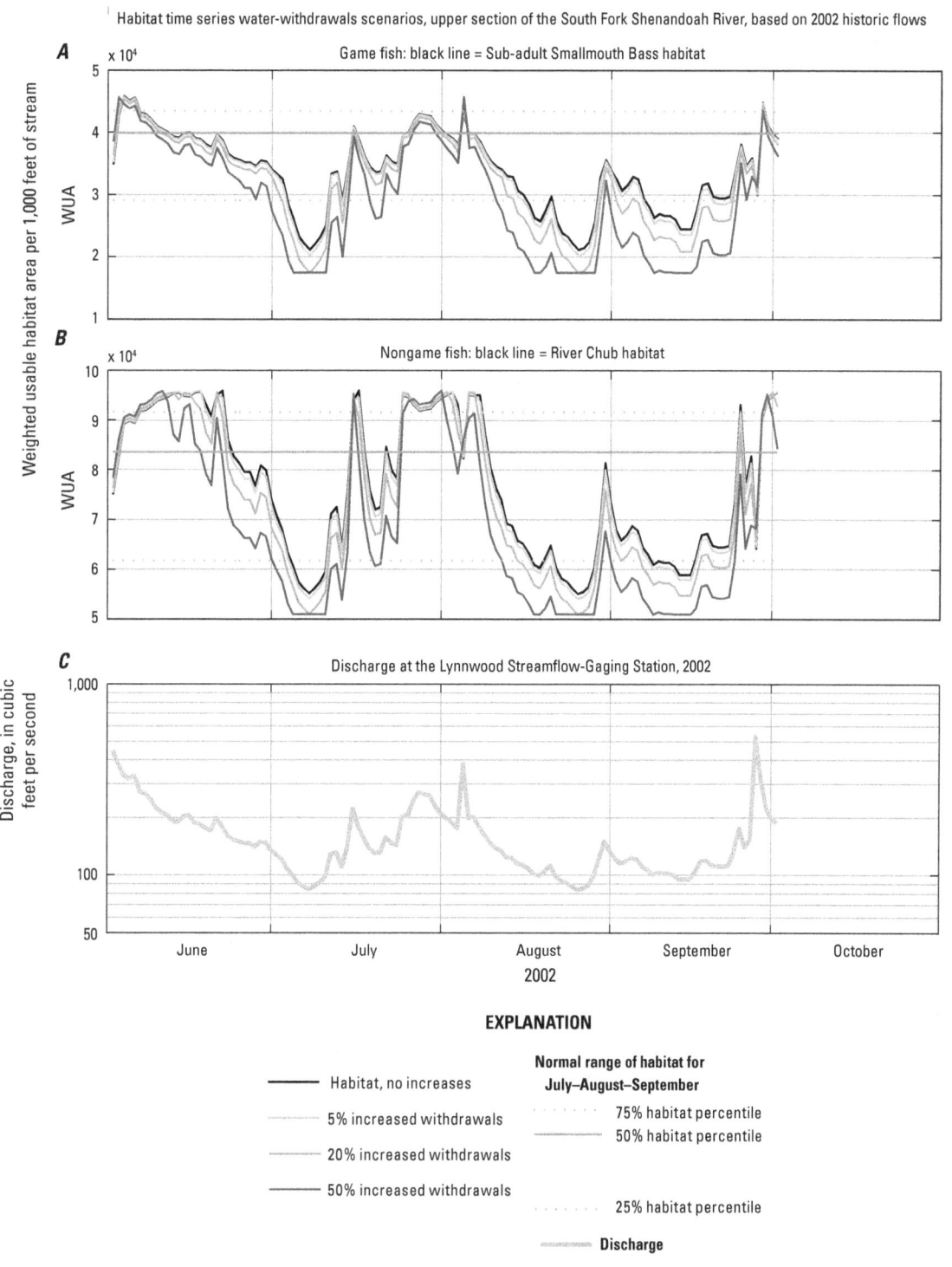

Figure 29.   Habitat time-series increased water-withdrawal scenarios for the upper section of the South Fork Shenandoah River near Lynnwood, Virginia, during 2002. *A*, sub-adult smallmouth bass weighted usable-habitat area with 5-, 20-, and 50-percent increase in water use; *B*, river chub weighted usable-habitat area with 5-, 20-, and 50-percent increase in water use; and *C*, daily mean discharge for the river near Lynnwood (01628500).

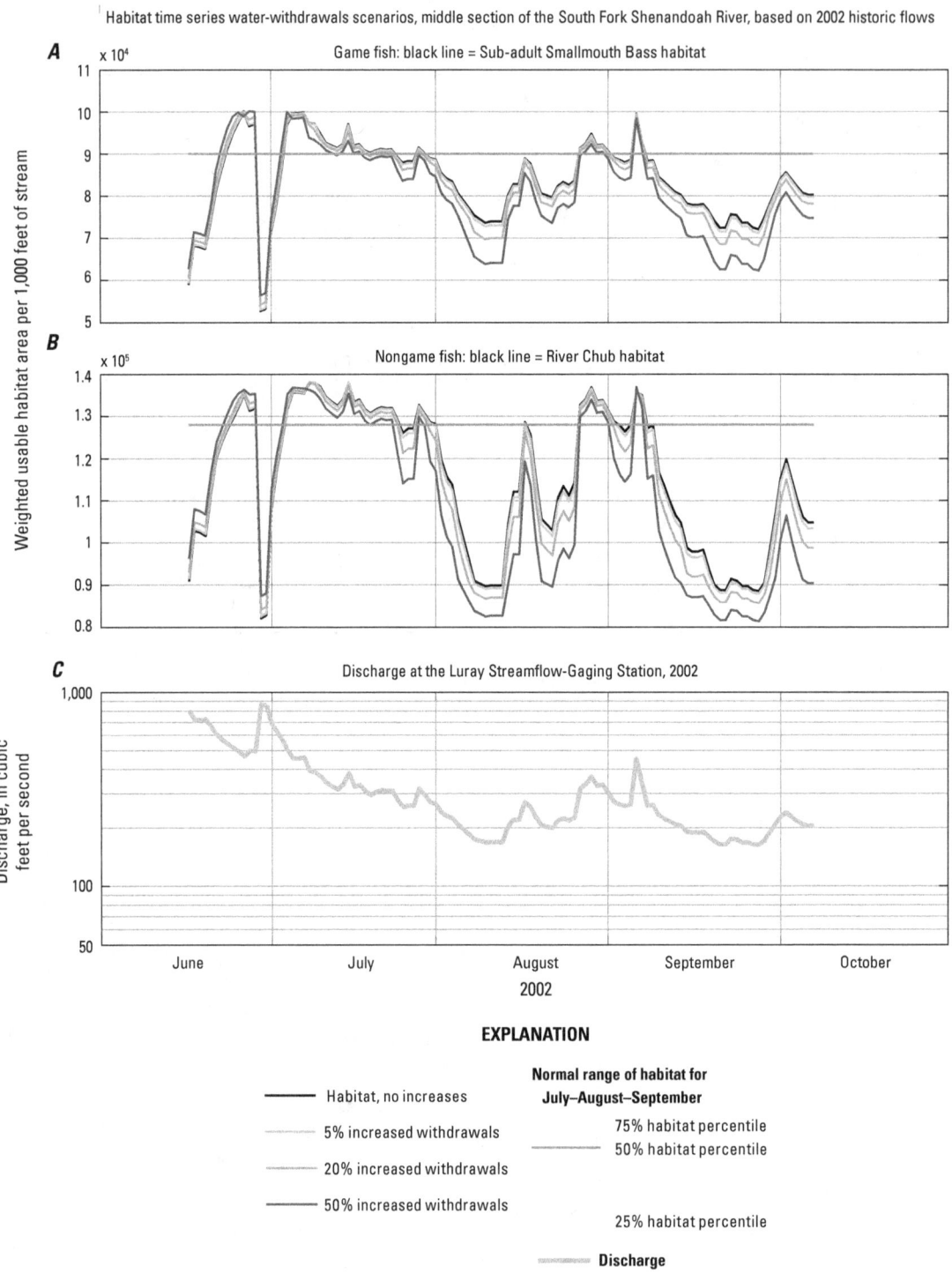

Figure 30. Habitat time-series increased water-withdrawal scenarios for the middle section of the South Fork Shenandoah River near Luray, Virginia, during 2002. *A*, sub-adult smallmouth bass weighted usable-habitat area with 5-, 20-, and 50-percent increase in water use; *B*, river chub weighted usable-habitat area with 5-, 20-, and 50-percent increase in water use; and *C*, daily mean discharge for the river near Luray (01629500).

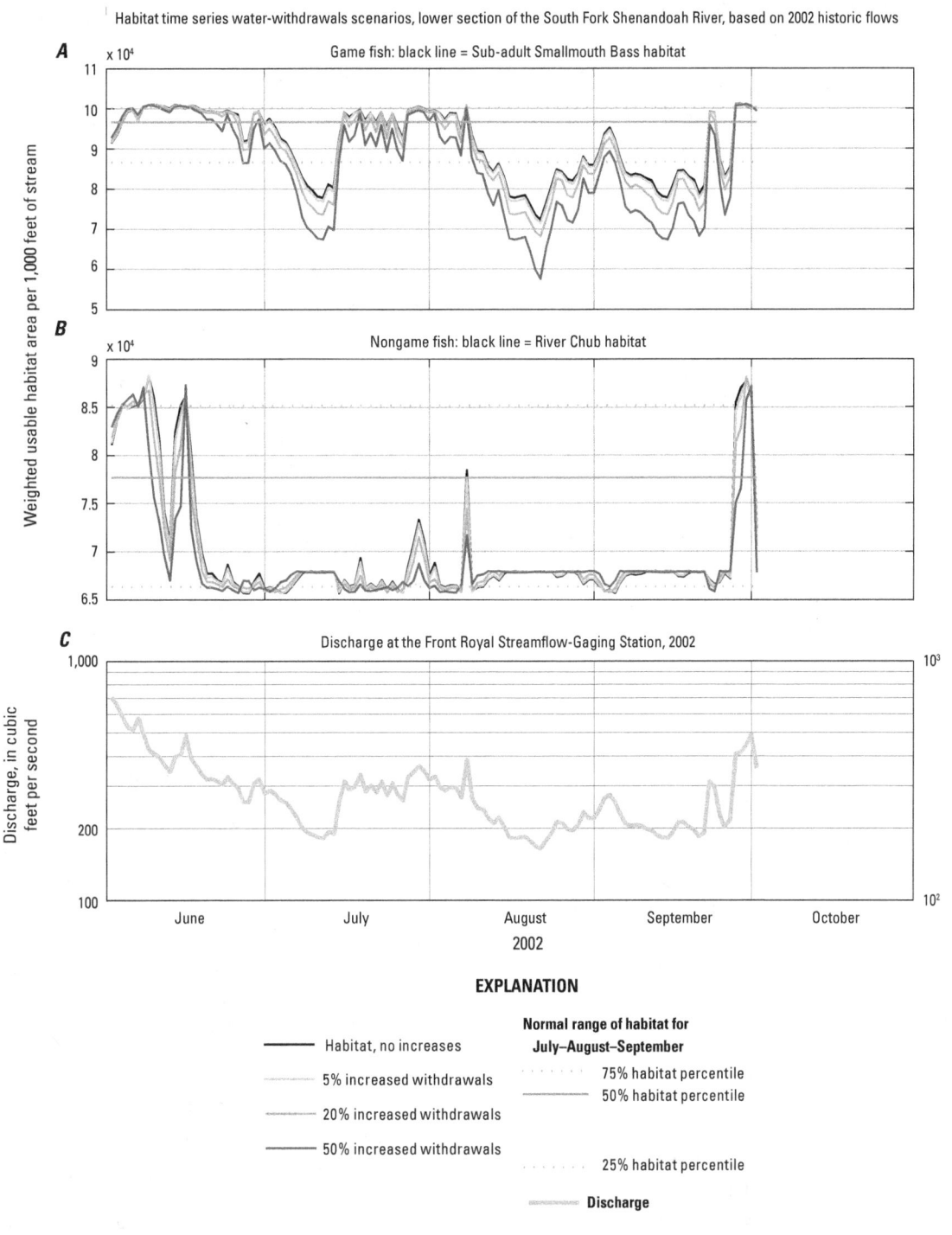

Figure 31.   Habitat time-series and water-withdrawal scenarios for the lower section of the South Fork Shenandoah River near Front Royal, Virginia, during 2002. *A,* sub-adult smallmouth bass weighted usable-habitat area with 5-, 20-, and 50-percent increase in water use; *B,* river chub weighted usable-habitat area with 5-, 20-, and 50-percent increase in water use; and *C,* daily mean discharge for the river at Front Royal (01631000).

Summary and Conclusions

The ecological habitat requirements of aquatic organisms and recreational streamflow requirements of the South Fork Shenandoah River were investigated by the U.S. Geological Survey in cooperation with the Central Shenandoah Valley Planning District Commission, the Northern Shenandoah Valley Regional Commission, and Virginia Commonwealth University beginning in 2005. The goal was to provide the counties and communities in the South Fork Basin information about water resources in the basin, the availability of water for fish habitat and canoeing, and the potential effects of withdrawals and conservation measures on the ecology, recreation, and water supply. This investigative report completes the modeling for the two major tributaries of the Shenandoah River, providing consistent results to planning district personnel toward effective drought preparation in the planning districts that span both watersheds. A key assumption of this investigation is that flow is a major determinant of physical habitat in rivers, which in turn is a major determinant of biotic composition. Another assumption is that physical habitat is a limiting factor for fish populations. This study incorporated critical flow components representing the annual flow regime as well as the summer low-flow period during July, August, and September (JAS) for three streamflow-gaging stations. Years with flows much lower than the normal range of flows in JAS (typically 10th percentile or lower) were classified as drought years.

Water-use data for 2005 were summarized for major tributaries of the South Fork, the North, Middle, and South Rivers for a total of 37.9 million gallons per day (Mgal/d). Water was withdrawn for the South Fork near Lynnwood (0.4 Mgal/d), Luray (3.5 Mgal/d), and Front Royal (2.4 Mgal/d). The cumulative total for the South Fork Shenandoah River surface-water withdrawals for 2005 was 44.2 Mgal/d. During the low-flow period, the surface-water withdrawals represent 12 to 19 percent of the median flow.

Mesohabitat data were mapped along the entire length of the South Fork for use in prioritization of hydraulic monitoring reaches and to weight modeling results to represent the habitats within the entire length of the South Fork. The mesohabitat data represent moderately large hydrogeomorphic habitat units within each stream, such as a riffle, run, or pool having relatively homogeneous channel characteristics. The overall makeup of habitat throughout the South Fork is 11.7-percent riffle, 52.6-percent run and 35.7-percent pool. These data were useful for summarizing the overall habitat availability for fish in the river and served as the basis for weighting of cross section habitat types in the habitat modeling phase of this study.

Four reaches of the South Fork were studied between Lynnwood (located downstream from the confluence of the North, Middle, and South Rivers) and Front Royal (located near the confluence of the North Fork). Standard methods were used to collect channel and floodplain topographic information, and at least five measurements of hydrologic data were taken over a range of streamflows which represented summer flow conditions. Measurements included water-surface level, water depth, water velocity, and discharge, which are relevant to both recreation and fish habitat, as well as substrate and cover characteristics, which are relevant to fish habitat.

Field-collected data were used to develop habitat suitability criteria (HSC) of fish in the South Fork. Optimal and marginal HSC were defined for fishes of the South Fork having observation data of 30 or larger with the exception of smallmouth bass, which had a sample size of only 18. Ranges of optimal habitat were defined as those used by the central 50 percent of the taxa or life stage sampled. Marginal habitats were those used by the fish outside the range of the central 50 percent, but within the central 80 percent of the taxa or life stage sampled. The HSC were developed for sub-adult and adult smallmouth bass (*Micropterus dolomieu*), juvenile and sub-adult redbreast sunfish (*Lepomis auritus*), *Cyprinella* spp., margined madtom (*Noturus insignis*), and river chub (*Nocomis micropogon*).

Flow and habitat modeling were completed using the program RHABSIM 3.0 for DOS and Windows. Field-measured flow calibration datasets were combined with the HSC to simulate available ecological and recreational habitat for 30 streamflows. This resulted in development of a functional relation between habitat and streamflow and is expressed in the form of weighted usable-habitat area (WUA) curves.

Modeling results for usable-habitat area for each fish species and canoeing suitability were compared to critical flow statistics, such as the normal range of flows, the 5th percentile flow for JAS flows, and the annual 7Q10 statistic to determine flows when habitat may be limited. In the Lynnwood section (upper section) the normal range of flows for JAS includes the maximum usable-habitat area for sub-adult redbreast sunfish, adult smallmouth bass, and sub-adult smallmouth bass. Lower than normal flows, however, provide greater habitat availability for smaller riffle-dwelling fish like *Cyprinella* spp., river chub, margined madtom, and juvenile redbreast sunfish. The Lynnwood study reach contains one riffle which could limit canoe passage, but model results indicate that a discharge of 460 cubic feet per second (ft³/s) could ensure that depths in the riffle are greater than or equal to 1-foot (ft) deep, sufficient for canoe passage. For ideal canoeing conditions, modeling results for Lynnwood indicate a discharge of 604 ft³/s up to 2,400 ft³/s.

For the Luray section (middle section) the normal range of flows for JAS includes the maximum usable habitat for all fish, except juvenile redbreast sunfish and sub-adult redbreast sunfish, which have maximum usable habitat lower than the 5th percentile flow and slightly lower than the 25th percentile flow, respectively. Despite the large range of maximum usable habitat among species, the 10th percentile flow (300 ft³/s) seems to maintain habitat availability for all species in the middle section. Kauffman Mill study reach has a high-gradient riffle that could limit canoe passage, but model results indicate that a discharge equal to 520 ft^3/s should provide an average depth of 1.3 ft, sufficient for canoe passage. For ideal canoeing conditions, modeling results for Luray indicate a discharge of 890 ft^3/s.

For the Front Royal (lower section) the normal range of flows for JAS includes the maximum usable habitat for all fish, except juvenile redbreast sunfish and sub-adult redbreast sunfish, which have maximum usable habitat lower than the 5th percentile flow and slightly lower than the 25th percentile flow, respectively. For pool and run-dwelling game fish like smallmouth bass and redbreast sunfish, habitat availability does not vary much from the normal range of flows for the low-flow period, down to the 5th percentile flow. Below the 5th percentile, habitat sharply decreases. For riffle-dwelling fish, the normal range of flows maintains habitat availability, and below the 25th percentile flow habitat remains below normal and steady. Canoeing through the Front Royal section takes the paddler through the widest channels on the South Fork and extensive sections of bedrock riffle like that found along the Thunderbird Farms study reach. Recreational habitat modeling results indicate that ideal canoeing conditions range from 831 up to 2,064 ft^3/s.

Habitat availability can be further analyzed by developing an association between habitat and streamflow-gaging stations on the South Fork that were in operation during previous droughts. This analysis should help identify species and habitats affected by drought. The results are interpretations of the weighted usable-habitat area curves and the historic flow record to create "time-series plots" of habitat and streamflow. The time-series associations can be ranked for the entire period of record for a streamgage to create a historic summary of habitat with a focus on the months of JAS. This allows the evaluation of daily habitat time-series data for a summer drought within the context of the normal habitat range, or the 25th to 75th percentile of habitat. Multiple historic summer drought low-flow periods were examined for each study site when data were available; the most extreme drought on record occurred in 2002, which represents worst-case conditions for each section.

Time-series results for drought years such as 2002 showed that extreme low-flow conditions less than the 5th percentile of flow for JAS corresponded to below-normal habitat availability for both game and nongame fish in the upper section of the river. During 2002, habitat availability for all species except juvenile redbreast sunfish decreased between 40 to 70 percent for a given species when flows decreased from 200 to 84 ft^3/s. For the middle section near Luray, time-series results from 2002 showed habitat area was below normal for nongame fish, such as margined madtom and river chub, whereas habitat area for game fish adult and sub-adult smallmouth bass remained within normal range. For comparison in 1999, habitat availability decreased slightly less than the median habitat percentile for sub-adult smallmouth bass, margined madtom, and river chub, but did not decrease below normal during that year's drought. In the middle section, as demonstrated by the 1999 drought, when

flows remain above the 5th percentile JAS flow, habitat availability is not expected to decrease outside the normal range of habitat. In the lower section near Front Royal, time-series results for adult smallmouth bass, sub-adult smallmouth bass, and margined madtom habitat for 2002 were below normal when flows were below the 10th percentile JAS flow. All other species of fish had habitat availability within the normal range for JAS.

Adequate flows for canoeing rarely occurred during the 2002 low-flow period. For instance, along the middle section of the South Fork, flows less than the 25th percentile flow for JAS did not provide adequate depth for passage through riffle habitats. Although recreation is certainly a consideration for water-resources management, when flows were far below the 25th percentile and decreasing, time-series results did not indicate that paddling conditions could be favorable even with conservation efforts, such as reduced water withdrawals.

Water-conservation scenarios representing 10- or 20-percent reduced water withdrawals resulted in minor increases in habitat availability for game fish for the 2002 drought simulation. For game fish, 50-percent water-withdrawal reduction resulted in habitat availability within the normal range for habitat in upper and middle river sections. For nongame fish such as river chub, a 20-percent withdrawal reduction resulted in habitat availability within the normal range for habitat in the upper and middle river sections. Water-withdrawal reduction scenarios simulated for 2002 for the lower section near Front Royal did not result in increased habitat availability for nongame fish.

Increased water-use scenarios representing a 5-percent increase in water withdrawals resulted in a slight reduction in habitat availability for the 2002 drought simulation; however, 20- and 50-percent increased withdrawals resulted in habitat availability substantially less than the 25th habitat percentile, or below normal. Habitat reductions were more pronounced when flows were lower than the 10th percentile flow for JAS. The results show that for normal or slightly dry years, increased water withdrawals are not likely to correspond with extensive habitat loss for game fish or nongame fish; however, during drought years, 20- to 50-percent increased water withdrawals may result in below normal habitat availability for game fish throughout the river and nongame fish in the upper and middle sections of the river. These simulations of rare historic drought conditions, such as those observed in 2002, serve as a baseline for development of ecological flow thresholds for drought planning.

References

Aadland, L.P., 1993, Stream habitat types—Their fish assemblages and relationship to flow: North American Journal of Fisheries Management, v. 12, p.790–806.

Aadland, L.P., Negua, M.T., Drewes, H.G., and Anderson, S.C., 1991, Microhabitat preferences of selected stream fishes and a community oriented approach to instream flow assessments: St. Paul, Minnesota Department of Fish and Wildlife, Section of Fisheries Investigational Report 406, 123 p.

Annear, T., Chisolm, I., Beecher, H., Locke, A., Aarestad, P., Coomer, C., Estes, C., Hunt, J., Jacobson, R., Jobsis, G., Kauffman, J., Marshall, J., Mayes, K., Smith, G., Wentworth, R., and Stalnaker, C., 2002, Instream flows for riverine resource stewardship (revised): Cheyenne, Wyo., Instream Flow Council, 268 p., 5 apps.

Arscott, D.B., Diettrich, J.C., Larned, S.T., and Schmidt, J., 2010, A framework for analyzing longitudinal and temporal variation in river flow and developing flow-ecology relationships: Journal of the American Water Resources Association, v. 46, no. 3, p. 541–553.

Austin, S.H., Krstolic, J.L., and Wiegand, Ute, 2011, Peak-flow characteristics of Virginia Streams: U.S. Geological Survey Scientific Investigations Report 2011–5144, 106 p., 3 tables and 2 apps. on CD.

Bain, M.B., and Brooke, H.E., 1985, A quantitative method for sampling riverine microhabitats by electrofishing: North American Journal of Fisheries Management, v. 5, p. 489–493.

Bovee, K.D, 1986, Development and evaluation of habitat suitability criteria for use in the instream flow incremental methodology: Instream Flow Information Paper 21: U.S. Fish and Wildlife Service Biological Report no. 86, v. 7, 235 p.

Bovee, K.D., 1997, Data collection procedures for the physical habitat simulation system, Fort Collins, Colorado: U.S. Geological Survey, 146 p., accessed March 17, 2011, at *http://www.mesc.usgs.gov/Products/Publications/pub_abstract.asp?PubID=20002*.

Bovee, K.D., Lamb, B.L., Bartholow, J.M., Stalnaker, C.B., Taylor, J., and Henriksen, J., 1998, Stream habitat analysis using the instream flow incremental methodology: U.S. Geological Survey Information and Technology Report 1998–0004, 130 p.

Bovee, K.D, and Zuboy, J.R. (eds.), 1988, Proceedings of a workshop on the development and evaluation of habitat suitability criteria: A compilation of papers and discussions presented at Colorado State University, Fort Collins, Colorado, December 8–12, 1986: U.S. Fish and Wildlife Service, 407 p.

Buchanan, T.J., and Somers, W.P., 1969, Discharge measurements at gaging stations: U.S. Geological Survey Techniques of Water-Resources Investigations, book 3, chap. A8, 65 p.

Bunn, S.E., and Arthington, A.H., 2002, Basic principles and the ecological consequences of altered flow regimes for aquatic biodiversity: Environmental Management, v. 30, p. 492–507.

Conover, W.J, 1980, Practical nonparametric statistics: New York, John Wiley, 493 p.

Daniel, W.W., 2005, Biostatistics: A foundation for analysis in the health sciences (8th ed.): New Jersey, John Wiley, 783 p.

Downriver Canoe Company, 2011, River conditions for canoeing: Accessed January 19, 2011, at *http://www.downriver.com/riverconditions*.

Freeman, M.C., Bowen, Z.H., and Crance, J.H., 1997, Transferability of habitat suitability criteria for fishes in warmwater streams: North American Journal of Fisheries Management, v. 17, p. 20–31.

Goldstein, R.M., 1978, Quantitative comparison of seining and underwater observation for stream fishery surveys: The Progressive Fish Culturist, v. 3, p. 108–111.

Haley, C.J., Hrezo, M.S., and Walker, W.R., 1989, Management of water resources during drought conditions: U.S. Geological Survey Water Supply Paper 2375, p. 147–156.

Harlow, G.E., Jr., Orndorff, R.C., Nelms, D.L., Weary, D.J., and Moberg, R.M., Jr., 2005, Hydrogeology and ground-water availability in the carbonate aquifer system of Frederick County, Virginia: U.S. Geological Survey Scientific Investigations Report 2005–5161, 30 p.

Harvey, C.A., and Eash, D.A., 1996, Description, instructions, and verification for Basinsoft, a computer program to quantify drainage-basin characteristics: U.S. Geological Survey Water- Resources Investigations Report 95–4287, 25 p.

Kenny, J.F., Barber, N.L., Hutson, S.S., Linsey, K.S., Lovelace, J.K., and Maupin, M.A., 2009, Estimated use of water in the United States in 2005: U.S. Geological Survey Circular 1344, 52 p.

Krstolic, J.L., 2006, Drainage basin delineations for selected USGS streamflow-gaging stations in Virginia: Metadata release, accessed at *http://water.usgs.gov/GIS/metadata/usgswrd/XML/ofr2006-1308_Drainage_Basin.xml*.

Krstolic, J.L., and Hayes, D.C., 2010, Physical habitat characteristics on the North and South Forks of the Shenandoah River, Virginia, in 2002–2007: U.S. Geological Survey Data Series 2010–539, accessed at url: *http://water.usgs.gov/GIS/metadata/usgswrd/XML/ds_539_MesoHabitat.xml.*

Krstolic, J.L., Hayes, D.C., and Ruhl, P.M., 2006, Physical habitat classification and instream flow modeling to determine habitat availability during low-flow periods, North Fork Shenandoah River, Virginia: U.S. Geological Survey Scientific Investigations Report 2006–5025, 63 p.

Larned, S.T., Arscott, D.B., Schmidt, J., and Diettrich, J.C., 2010, A framework for analyzing longitudinal and temporal variation in river flow and developing flow-ecology relationships: Journal of the American Water Resources Association, v. 46, no. 3, p. 541–553.

Lovelace, J.K., 2009a, Methods for estimating water withdrawals for aquaculture in the United States, 2005: U.S. Geological Survey Scientific Investigations Report 2009–5042, 13 p.

Lovelace, J.K., 2009b, Methods for estimating water withdrawals for livestock in the United States, 2005: U.S. Geological Survey Scientific Investigations Report 2009–5041, 7 p.

Lovelace, J.K., 2009c, Methods for estimating water withdrawals for mining in the United States, 2005: U.S. Geological Survey Scientific Investigations Report 2009–5053, 7 p.

Maki-Petays, A., Huusko, A., Erkinaro, J., and Muotka, T., 2002, Transferability of habitat suitability criteria of juvenile Atlantic Salmon (*Salmo solar*): Canadian Journal of Fisheries and Aquatic Sciences, v. 59, p. 218–228.

Nelms, D.L., and Moberg, R.M., Jr., 2010, Hydrogeology and groundwater availability in Clarke County, Virginia: U.S. Geological Survey Scientific Investigations Report 2010–5112, 119 p.

Morgan, B.A., Eaton, L.S., and Wieczorek, G.F., 2004, Pleistocene and Holocene colluvial fans and terraces in the Blue Ridge region of Shenandoah National Park, Virginia: U.S. Geological Survey Open-File Report 03–410, 25 p.

Mueller, D.S., and Wagner, C.R., 2009, Measuring discharge with acoustic Doppler current profilers from a moving boat: U.S. Geological Survey Techniques and Methods, book 3, chap. A22, 72 p. (Also available at *http://pubs.water.usgs.gov/tm3a22.*)

Multi-Resolution Land Characteristics Consortium, 2001, National Land Cover Database 2001: Accessed October 2010 at *http://www.mrlc.gov/nlcd.php.*

Paybins, K.S., 2008, Basin characteristics for selected streamflow-gaging stations in and near West Virginia, U.S. Geological Survey Open-File Report 2008–1087, 9 p.

Persinger, J.W., 2003, Developing habitat suitability criteria for individual species and habitat guilds in the Shenandoah River Basin: Master thesis, Virginia Polytechnic Institute and State University.

Petts, G.E., 2009, Instream flow science for sustainable river management: Journal of the American Water Resources Association, v. 45, no. 5, p. 1071–1086.

Power, M.E., and Matthews, W.J., 1983. Algae-grazing minnows (*Campostoma anomalum*), piscivorous bass (*Micropterus* spp.), and the distribution of attached algae in a small prairie-margin stream: Berlin, Oecologia, v. 60, p. 328–332.

Ramey, R.C., 2009, Habitat suitability criteria for fishes of the South Fork of the Shenandoah River and an investigation into observer effects associated with two techniques of underwater observation: Master thesis, Virginia Commonwealth University, 123 p.

Rantz, S.E., and others, 1982, Measurement and computation of streamflow—Volume 1: U.S. Geological Survey Water-Supply Paper 2175, 284 p.

Searcy, J.K., 1969, Flow-duration curves, manual of hydrology—Part 2, Low-flow techniques: U.S. Geological Survey Water-Supply Paper 1542-A, 33 p.

SonTek YSI, Incorporated, 2006, FlowTracker, FT Brochure 10/06, Rev. 4—Oxford Group: Accessed May 2012, at *http://www.sontek.com/flowtracker.php.*

Stalnaker, C.B., 1979, The use of habitat structure preferenda for establishing flow regimes necessary for maintenance of fish habitat, *in* Ward, J.V., and Stanford, J.A., eds., The ecology of regulated streams: New York, Plenum Press, p. 321–338.

Swain, L.A., Mesko, T.O., and Hollyday, E.F., 2004, Summary of the hydrogeology of the valley and ridge, Blue Ridge, and Piedmont Physiographic Provinces in the Eastern United States: U.S. Geological Survey Professional Paper 1422–A, 31 p.

Tharme, R.E., 2003, A global perspective on environmental flow assessment: Emerging trends in the development and application of environmental flow methodologies for rivers: River Research and Applications, v. 19, p. 397–441.

Thomas, J.A., and Bovee, K.D., 1993, Application and testing of a procedure to evaluate transferability of habitat suitability criteria: Regulated Rivers: Research and Management, v. 8, p. 285–294.

Thomas R. Payne and Associates, 1998, User's manual: RHABSIM [Riverine Habitat Simulation software] 2.0 for Dos and Windows, variously paged.

Thurow, Russell F, 1994, Underwater methods for study of salmonids in the Intermountain West: U.S. Forest Service General Technical Report 307.

Turnipseed, D.P., and Sauer, V.B., 2010, Discharge measurements at gaging stations: U.S. Geological Survey Techniques and Methods, book 3, chap. A8, 87 p. (Also available at *http://pubs.usgs.gov/tm/tm3-a8/.*)

Vadas, R.L., Jr., 1992, Seasonal habitat use, species associations, and assemblage structure of forage fishes in Goose Creek, Northern Virginia: II. Mesohabitat patterns, Journal of Freshwater Ecology, v. 7, p. 149–164.

Vadas, R.L., Jr., and Orth, D.J., 1998, Use of physical variables to discriminate visually determined mesohabitat types in North American streams, Rivers, v. 6, no. 3, p 143–159.

Virginia Department of Game and Inland Fisheries, 2011, Shenandoah River-South Fork, available at: *http://www.dgif. virginia.gov/fishing/waterbodies/display.asp?id=173.*

Virginia Department of Mines, Minerals, and Energy, 2005, Digital representation of the1993 geologic map of Virginia: Charlottesville, Va., Division of Mineral Resources, Vector digital data, Publication 174, scale 1:500,000.

Waddle, T.J., ed., 2001, PHABSIM [Physical Habitat Simulation model] for Windows—User's manual and exercises: Fort Collins, Colo.: U.S. Geological Survey Open-File Report 01–340, 288 p., accessed March 17, 2011, at *http:// www.mesc.usgs.gov/Products/Publications/pub_abstract. asp?PubID=15000.*

Walker, W.R., Hrezo, M.S., and Haley, C.J., 1991, Management of water resources for drought conditions, *in* Paulson, R.W., Chase, E.B., Roberts, R.S., and Moody, D.W., compilers, National Water Summary 1988–89—Hydrologic events and floods and droughts: U.S. Geological Survey Water-Supply Paper 2375, p. 147–156.

Yager, R.M., Southworth, Scott, and Voss, C.I., 2008, Simulation of ground-water flow in the Shenandoah Valley, Virginia and West Virginia, using variable-direction anisotropy in hydraulic conductivity to represent bedrock structure: U.S. Geological Survey Scientific Investigations Report 2008–5002, 54 p.

Zappia, Humbert, and Hayes, D.C., 1998, A demonstration of the instream flow incremental methodology, Shenandoah River, Virginia: U.S. Geological Survey Water-Resources Investigations Report 98–4157, 24 p.

Appendixes

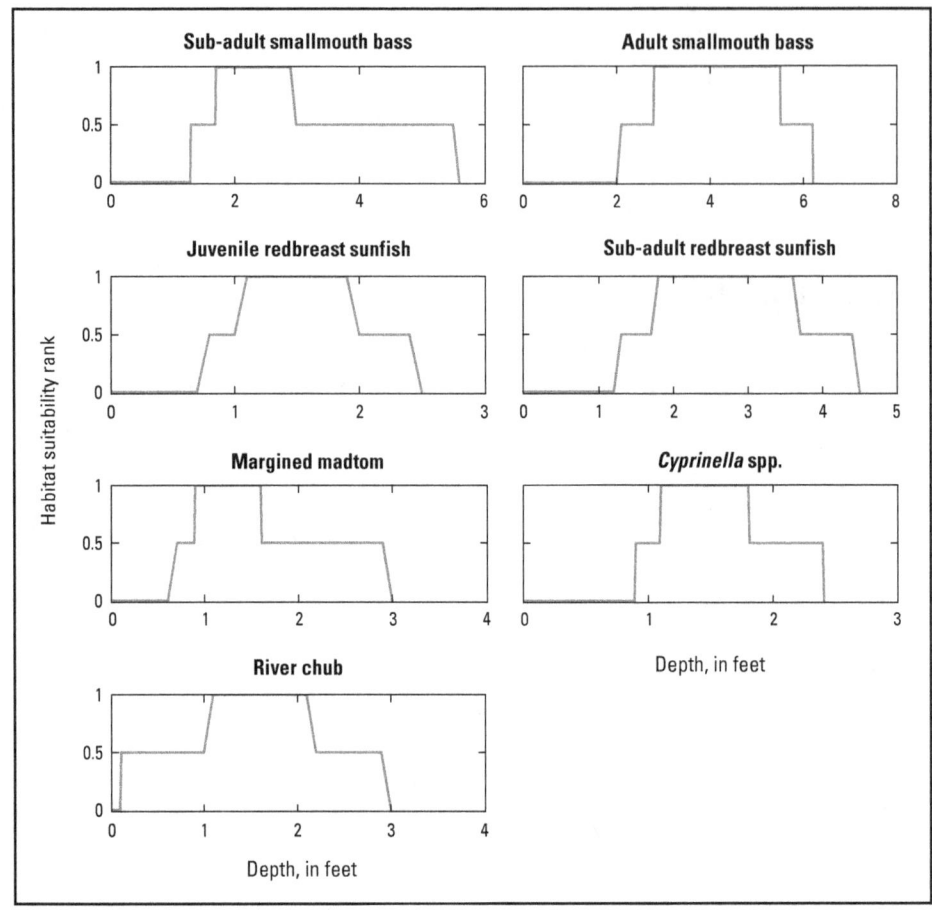

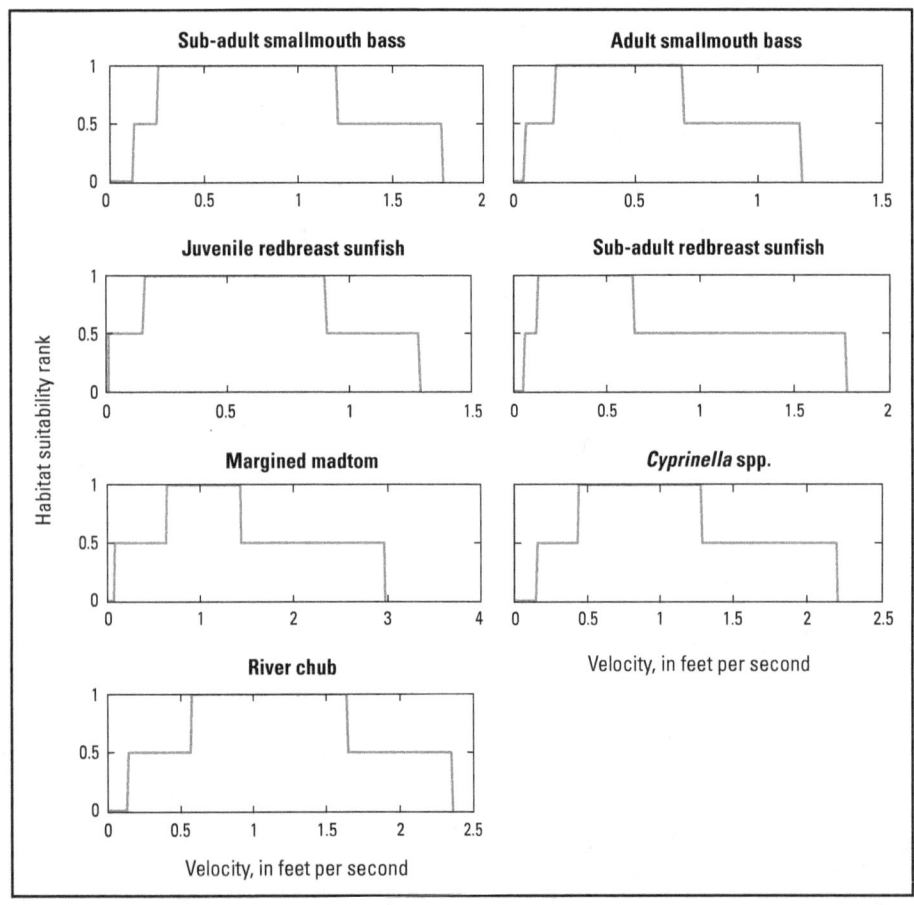

Appendix 1. Fish habitat suitability criteria for depth, velocity, and substrate characteristics on the south Fork Shenandoan River, Virginia. Substrate codes are listed in table 8.

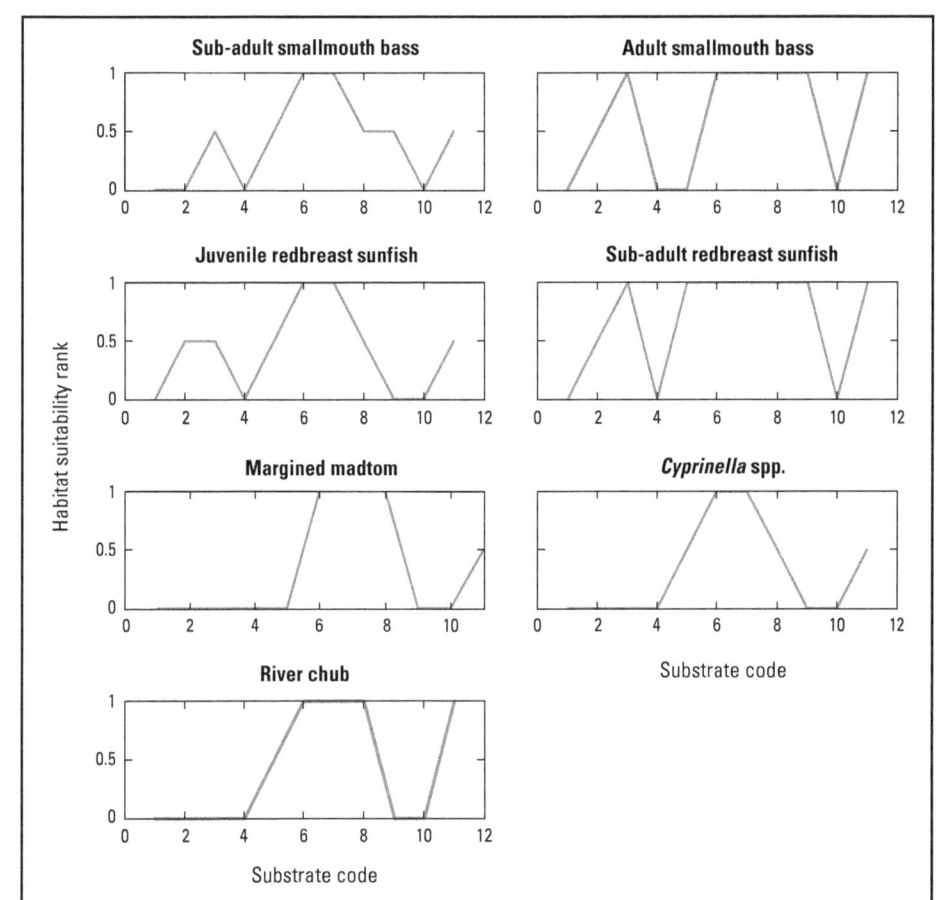

Appendix 1. Fish habitat suitability criteria for depth, velocity, and substrate characteristics on the south Fork Shenandoan River, Virginia. Substrate codes are listed in table 8.—Continued

Appendix 2.   River habitat simulation (RHABSIM) model-calibration data from the hydraulic data-collection reaches on the South Fork Shenandoah River, Virginia.

[Calculated discharge is an RHABSIM calculated value. SZF, stage zero flow; WSL, water-surface level; slope, average water-surface slope for all discharges measured; verticals, number of measurement points along the transect; ND, no data collected]

Transect	Observed WSL,[1] feet	Simulated WSL, feet	Reach calibration discharge,[1] ft³/s	Model-calculated discharge, ft³/s	Verti-cals	Transect weighting factor	Slope,[1] percent	SZF,[1] feet	Average depth, feet	Wetted width, feet	Velocity mean, ft/s
					Lynnwood						
	1,015.03	1,015.04	181	177.15					1.36	168.20	0.67
	1,015.12	1,015.12	221	228.66					1.42	169.77	0.86
1	1,015.78	1,015.79	725	769.61	35	0	0.0039	1,012.4	1.91	188.20	1.84
	1,015.89	1,015.88	780	809.88					1.93	196.50	1.74
	1,016.36	1,016.36	1,132	1,331.46					2.32	204.62	2.44
	1,014.28	1,014.28	181	140.94					0.65	137.93	1.13
	1,014.35	1,014.35	221	159.66					0.71	141.12	1.25
2	1,015.31	1,015.31	725	665.00	33	0.25	0.00340	1,012.31	1.51	162.41	2.46
	1,015.38	1,015.38	780	748.39					1.56	163.99	2.69
	1,015.86	1,015.86	1,132	1,363.80					1.93	175.13	3.80
	1,014.11	1,014.02	181	273.50					1.19	166.91	0.88
	1,014.13	1,014.13	221	278.99					1.20	167.05	0.93
3	1,014.82	1,014.89	725	851.86	37	0.5	0.00100	1,011.58	1.84	172.20	2.08
	1,014.96	1,014.95	780	948.66					1.98	172.99	2.21
	1,015.41	1,015.27	1,132	1,352.33					2.40	175.52	2.78
	1,014.03	1,013.94	181	188.28					1.76	183.49	0.58
	1,014.04	1,014.04	221	237.00					1.78	183.68	0.72
4	1,014.74	1,014.80	725	774.42	36	0.62	0.00040	1,011.57	2.39	191.27	1.59
	1,014.86	1,014.85	780	814.84					2.49	192.52	1.61
	1,015.29	1,015.15	1,132	1,250.16					2.87	196.35	2.04
	1,014.01	1,013.93	181	181.17					1.74	169.99	0.62
	1,014.03	1,014.03	221	198.69					1.75	170.15	0.68
5	1,014.74	1,014.78	725	748.76	31	1	0.00040	1,010.81	2.18	195.36	1.53
	1,014.84	1,014.83	780	841.49					2.27	195.69	1.67
	1,015.26	1,015.12	1,132	1,225.79					2.67	197.17	2.08
					Riverbend Pool						
	905.13	905.12	271	262.99					5.69	243.41	0.15
	905.47	905.45	380	284.01					6.00	245.00	0.15
1	905.79	905.80	554	553.97	29	0	0.00005	895.58	6.28	246.47	0.31
	906.12	906.13	962	1,142.06					6.57	247.97	0.61
	906.51	906.51	1,187	1,308.75					6.91	249.79	0.56
	905.12	905.12	271	240.65					7.98	218.77	0.11
	905.46	905.45	380	303.92					8.24	220.89	0.14
2	905.79	905.80	554	564.91	31	0.2	0.00004	893.30	8.49	223.00	0.26
	906.11	906.13	962	1,005.27					8.74	225.03	0.50
	906.50	906.51	1,187	1,073.40					9.02	227.80	0.52
	905.12	905.12	271	191.85					8.33	205.60	0.10
	905.44	905.44	380	269.30					8.55	208.16	0.15
3	905.79	905.79	554	609.68	30	0.6	0.00004	890.50	8.78	210.92	0.29
	906.11	906.11	962	1,018.35					9.00	213.46	0.49
	906.49	906.49	1,187	1,238.59					9.24	216.41	0.58
					Kauffman Mill						
	723.02	723.01	358	ND[2]					2.31	216.93	ND[2]
	723.27	723.27	631	ND[2]					2.52	219.80	ND[2]
0	723.50	723.50	890	923.20	34	0	0.0032	720.54	2.72	222.57	1.52
	723.93	723.93	1,540	ND[2]					2.98	235.67	ND[2]
	724.21	724.21	2,087	2,193.99					3.18	242.73	2.48

Appendix 2. River habitat simulation (RHABSIM) model-calibration data from the hydraulic data-collection reaches on the South Fork Shenandoah River, Virginia.—Continued

[Calculated discharge is an RHABSIM calculated value. SZF, stage zero flow; WSL, water-surface level; slope, average water-surface slope for all discharges measured; verticals, number of measurement points along the transect; ND, no data collected]

Transect	Observed WSL,[1] feet	Simulated WSL, feet	Reach calibration discharge,[1] ft³/s	Model-calculated discharge, ft³/s	Verti-cals	Transect weighting factor	Slope,[1] percent	SZF,[1] feet	Average depth, feet	Wetted width, feet	Velocity mean, ft/s
					Kauffman Mill—Continued						
	722.43	722.43	358	489.61					1.02	288.30	1.54
	722.90	722.90	631	974.65					1.47	292.01	2.23
1	723.12	723.12	890	1,484.73	49	0.11	0.0036	720.54	1.68	294.65	2.80
	723.60	723.60	1,540	ND[2]					2.00	318.91	ND[2]
	723.82	723.82	2,087	ND[2]					2.19	324.76	ND[2]
	721.47	721.40	358	332.82					1.44	307.57	0.73
	721.70	721.70	631	609.83					1.67	308.39	1.19
2	721.91	721.90	890	880.80	46	0.67	0.0052	718.61	1.88	309.15	1.58
	722.28	722.27	1,540	1,879.31					2.23	310.48	2.77
	722.65	722.51	2,087	2,460.99					2.60	311.82	3.08
	720.64	720.58	358	322.18					2.01	231.00	0.67
	720.88	720.88	631	767.82					2.22	234.73	1.40
3	720.99	721.08	890	1,102.87	37	0.75	0.004	717.33	2.30	236.60	1.94
	721.42	721.42	1,540	1,814.10					2.66	243.88	2.60
	722.04	721.62	2,087	2,439.50					3.21	249.86	2.90
	720.54	720.48	358	298.37					2.15	216.53	0.59
	720.79	720.79	631	739.99					2.36	220.55	1.29
4	720.94	720.99	890	1,067.11	40	1	0.0016	716.8	2.38	232.76	1.58
	721.34	721.34	1,540	1,745.59					2.73	237.13	2.32
	721.95	721.55	2,087	2,338.24					3.26	243.75	2.64
					Thunderbird Farms						
	494.42	494.42	327	328.17					4.47	305.22	0.23
	494.46	494.44	349	406.40					4.50	305.47	0.28
1	494.46	494.47	404	408.64	49	0	0.0002	492.73	4.50	305.47	0.29
	495.17	495.17	1,123	ND[2]					5.15	309.76	0.00
	495.96	495.96	2,064	2,156.24					5.88	312.76	1.09
	494.42	494.41	327	340.71					5.79	306.70	0.18
	494.46	494.44	349	382.01					5.83	306.82	0.20
2	494.47	494.47	404	ND[2]	41	0.0	0.00010	492.73	5.84	306.85	0.00
	495.17	495.16	1,123	1,168.77					6.49	309.00	0.55
	495.93	495.95	2,064	2,145.55					7.20	311.34	0.91
	494.42	494.41	327	309.95					2.20	364.05	0.37
	494.44	494.43	349	390.91					2.22	364.22	0.47
3	494.47	494.46	404	394.86	53	0.8	0.00020	492.73	2.25	364.48	0.46
	495.12	495.13	1,123	1,161.46					2.86	370.04	1.08
	495.87	495.88	2,064	2,155.15					3.57	374.89	1.57
	494.28	494.28	327	387.19					0.83	370.07	1.24
	494.32	494.32	349	354.54					0.87	370.52	1.06
4	494.36	494.36	404	374.90	55	1	0.0009	492.73	0.91	370.98	1.14
	494.97	494.97	1,123	1,212.53					1.50	377.11	2.12
	495.66	495.66	2,064	2,307.17					2.16	383.79	2.78

[1]Value collected from field measurements.

[2]No velocity dataset collected for this water-surface level.

For information regarding this publication, contact:
  Director
  U.S. Geological Survey
  Virginia Water Science Center
  1730 East Parham Road
  Richmond, VA 23228
  http://va.water.usgs.gov

Prepared by:
  USGS Science Publishing Network
  Raleigh Publishing Service Center
  3916 Sunset Ridge Road
  Raleigh, NC 27607

USGS publishing staff:
  Twila Darden Wilson, Managing editor and layout
  James E. Banton, Illustration assistance and cover